Girl's Talk

REVIVING MARRIAGES & PREPARING
SINGLES

Dr. Jennifer Wiseman

Ladies on Fire Ministries
93 Camberwell Station Road
London, England SE5 9JJ
www.ladiesonfire.org
Email: drjennifer@ladiesonfire.org
Tel: 44 207 738 3668 (UK)
Tel: 1 347 708 1449 (USA)

CONTENTS

ACKNOWLEDGEMENTS

I give all the Glory to God for everything He has done. His Wisdom, Empowerment, Revelation knowledge giving me such a message as at time like this.

My deepest love and appreciation to my Husband, who is my Friend, Pastor, Coach, Mentor, Bishop and my prayer partner, Bishop Climate, who have played a great part by encouraging me all the way.

To my precious daughter Summer, full of confidence. I will always love you. I'm proud of your gift and wisdom as a young mighty woman of God. Thank you for your encouragement towards this book.

Climate Junior my boy so sweet, tender, brave, strong, and Anointed youth preacher. I thank you too for your encouragement in this book. Grace beautiful and adorable, with an Angelic voice I thank you for praising and worshiping across the room while I was writing the book, has also played a role in my book.

Finally, my Baby Sunshine, beautiful princess, you are adorable, cute and gifted to calm mummy with more love. Sunshine it's like you understood my passion in this book. One year and six months old. She remained quiet, freeing me to write this book in a unique way. I thank my kids for giving me space to write this book.

My sincere appreciation to all ladies on fire committees, you have been a source of encouragement, strength, inspiration and standing with me to see that this message goes to the whole world.

To all our TKC pastors, ministers, leaders, precious members, Partners in the whole world for your fellowship and believing the vision that God has given to us (Bishop and me). You have really encouraged us to go for further in our spiritual life.

All of our precious intercessors that have been encouraging and praying Non-stop seeing this book as an answer to all women in the world.

Finally special thanks to Minister Chido Madziko for editing and lining up my book. Thank you so much, God bless you.

INTRODUCTION

The Bible says, "The Lord gives the word [of power]; the women who bear and publish [the news] are a great host." (Psalm 68:11 AMPC)

The reason why am writing this book, I truly believe with all my heart that I am that women God has called, chosen and anointed to bear and publish what He has placed in my heart and share with other women from all walks of life. I believe am anointed and ordained by God to share with others the wisdom from above.

Girls Talk started in Scotland in 2013, whereby I was meeting married women once a month, sharing God wisdom, knowledge, and empowering them to enjoy their marriages. It began by teaching women how to pray for their husbands, kids, and having a family vision. I believe that when we have happy wives, we have happy husbands, happy children, happy homes, happy churches, happy communities, and happy nations. Happy wives creates happy atmosphere.

Girls talk is not about just talking, but it's about putting into practice what you are learning and obtaining tangible results which transform and revive marriages.

God is giving you knowledge, put it into practice. Build a beautiful marriage by paying attention to the details —to feed the bedroom. Girls Talk is the answer to your questions.

We have Girls Talk for temporary single ladies, preparing singles for successful marriages.

Girls Talk for married women, real talk, that revives marriages.

Now Girls Talk is live in 20 countries and 4 continents.

1. Scotland
2. England
3. Italy
4. USA
5. Canada
6. Australia
7. Namibia
8. Ireland
9. South Africa
10. Kenya
11. Sweden
12. New Zealand
13. Zimbabwe
14. Botswana
15.Ghana
16. Guyana
17. Germany
18. Tanzania
19. Nigeria
20. Netherlands

A GLOBAL WORD FOR ENCOURAGEMENT TO GIRLS TALK

"I am very pleased to announce that Girls talk was officially launched by Dr Jennifer in Bulawayo, city of Kings and Queens on Saturday 27 August 2016. The group was well attended, there were 95 ladies, there were old ladies, middle aged women, as well as young women.

The ladies and the grannies had a great experience of Girls talk, they listened attentively and at the end of the session, they asked questions and Dr Jennifer was able to answer all their questions. As you well know that girls talk can also, of course, provide useful information that covers broad feminine aspects/areas as well as giving further motivation for the audience. Girl's talk was an eye opener to all the ladies that attended and I am pretty sure that will spread the news about girls talk. They relinquished the knowledge that was given to them. Most people endorsed Girls talk and they want it to take place regularly.

There was a widow who came to the GIRLS TALK meeting, she had her wedding ring from her husband who died long time ago, she had tried to remove the ring for many years but it was all in vain. But her ring came out when she attended the Girls talk session.

Mama Dr Jennifer, we are very grateful, as ever, for your time, constructive answers that are most positive in our time. We are very proud of the way you integrated with us in a new environment and your passion in helping to set the ladies free. We did not have enough of Girls talk, please call again soon. God bless you and thank you."

A VIRTUOUS WIFE

Many of you women have been asking me, "What does that famous book of the Bible, the book of Proverbs, that seems to be so full of wisdom for every area of our lives has to say about us women?" Well, let me tell you ladies, God loves you very much, because there is a whole chapter in the book of Proverbs dedicated to just one woman—the Proverbs Chapter 31 Woman. How awesome is that! I have read this chapter through and through countless times, and because I have a passion to impart wisdom to women from all walks of life, I simply had to find all the goodness I can glean from this chapter. What I gathered is simply amazing!

I found TWELVE INCREDIBLE CHARACTERISTICS OF THIS Noble WOMAN, and that is what I am going to share with you. I pray that each and every one of you ladies reading this book will desire to become a PROVERBS 31 WOMEN (Proverbs 31:10-31).

1. VALUE: She is a noble (virtuous) woman who is worth far more than rubies. She is precious.

2. MARITAL RELATIONSHIP: Her husband has full confidence in her.

3. RESPECT: She brings him good, not harm, all the days of her life.

4. DILIGENCE (Hard work): She works with eager hands and does not eat the bread of idleness. She sets about her work vigorously.

5. THE FAMILY: She watches over the affairs of her household. She gets up while it is still night; she provides food for her family.

6. THE HOME: She makes coverings for her bed; she is clothed in fine linen and purple.

7. HONOUR TO HER HUSBAND: Because of her, the husband is respected at the city gate, where he takes his seat among the elders of the land.

8. GENEROSITY AND HOSPITALITY: She opens her arms to the poor and extends her hands to the needy.

9. SPEECH (Conversation): She speaks with wisdom, and faithful instruction is on her tongue.

10. CHILDREN: Her children arise and call her blessed – She is respected and valued by her children.

11. HUSBAND: Her husband also praises her and says, "Many women do noble things, but you surpass them all." Her husband values and respects her.

12. HER REPUTATION: Charm is deceptive, and beauty is fleeting; but a woman who fears the LORD is to be praised. Honour her for all that her hands have done, and let her works

bring her praise at the city gate. Her living testimony and her hard work causes people to respect her.

HOW TO REMAIN A SHE-EAGLE IN THE MIDST OF STORMS

My beloved Daughter, life is full of perplexing situations that often leave us wondering what to do or where to turn to. In our eyes some situations look hopeless but that is just the lie of the devil to make us lose focus. We need to have an eagle mentality of soaring up against the storm and never hiding away from them. Eagles are known to combat storms and fly against strong winds and still manage to overcome. The fiercer the storm is, the higher they fly. They are also known to be patient birds. That's why we need to emulate them.

"There are three things that are too amazing for me, for I do not understand: the way of an eagle in the sky." (Proverbs 30:18-19). As we get into prayer, I want you to believe and receive power to soar to great heights in the midst of storms just like an eagle.

1. Put on the full armour of God and begin to welcome the presence of God. Ask Him to have His way, remember you, take over the affairs of your life.

2. Pray that God will give you strength to stand on His word regardless of what is happening. That you will wait on Him to the end. He gives strength to the weary and increases the power of the weak. Even the youth grow tired and weary and the young men stumble and fall, but those who hope in

the Lord will renew their strength. They will soar on wings like eagles, they will run and not grow weary, they will walk and not faint." (Isaiah 40:29-31). You will not waiver nor shake, you will make it in Jesus' name.

3. Pray against the spirit of fear that makes you focus on the problem rather than God. Bind every spirit of fear in Jesus' name. You will overcome. Exodus 19:4 says, "you have seen what I did to Egyptians, carried you on eagle's wings brought you to myself.

4. Pray against all principalities and powers of darkness which are standing in your way and stopping you from achieving your potential. Bind them in Jesus' name. Command them to die by fire. Revelation 22:14 says, "The woman was given wings of a great Eagle so that she might fly to the place proposed for her in the desert where she would be taken care of for a time, a half out of the serpents reach."

5. Pray for the deliverance of God from that attack. Ask God to remember and deliver you.

Like an eagle that stirs up its nest and hovers over its young, that spreads its wings to catch them and carries them on its points. The Lord alone led them no foreign god was with him.

(Deuteronomy 32-11-12)

6. Begin to thank God because you have overcome. You are a SHE-Eagle. You have come out victorious and you will remain victorious in Jesus' name.

You are an overcomer in Jesus Name. YOU ARE A SHE EAGLE.

You need to practice the following points; a hunter's greatest power over its prey is seeing it first. Because eagles see their prey first, they gain an immediate tactical advantage by being able to choose when and from which angle they approach their target.

What if you saw your life circumstances and goals as your prey? What if you anticipated the things that would happen as a result of your actions? That gives you the advantage of adjusting your approach. Things do happen to us without us knowing sometimes, but more often than not, the direction we take determines what we'll receive.

EAGLES FLY ALONE AND ABOVE
Eagles fly alone and at high altitudes. They don't fly with sparrows or other small birds. Keep good company. Be a she eagle. Don't walk with corrupted friends.

Psalm 1:1 "Blessed is the one who does not walk in step with the wicked or stand in the way that sinners take or sit in the company of mockers,"

EAGLES HAVE A STRONG VISION
Eagles have 20/20 vision. They are able to see far. Have the ability to visualise and make prompt decisions. They can see a fresh rabbit from 1000ft. Write your vision down

Habakkuk 2:2 "And the Lord answered me, and said, Write the vision, and make it plain upon tables, that he may run that readeth it."

EAGLES DO NOT EAT DEAD THINGS

They always feed on fresh prey. Do not rely on your past success, keep looking for new frontiers to conquer. Vultures eat and can smell a dying animal even before time. Don't be a vulture but be a She Eagle.

Ezekiel 3:3-4 "Then he said to me, "Son of man, eat this scroll I am giving you and fill your stomach with it." So I ate it, and it tasted as sweet as honey in my mouth. He then said to me: "Son of man, go now to the people of Israel and speak my words to them."

EAGLES LOVES THE STORM

The storm assures that the eagle will soar high. Face your challenges, knowing that these will make you emerge stronger and better than you were. Every day in every way you are becoming better and better. She- eagles fly above every level of challenges.

Matthew 8:27 "The men were amazed and asked, "What kind of man is this? Even the winds and the waves obey him!"

EAGLES TEST BEFORE TRUST

Test the loyalty and commitment of your friends and leaders in your team.

2 Corinthians 8:8 "I am not commanding you, but I want to test the sincerity of your love by comparing it with the earnestness of others."

EAGLES PREPARE FOR TRAINING

Eagles prepare and positions themselves by removing the feathers and soft grass in the nest so that the young ones get uncomfortable in preparation for flying. Leave your comfort zone - there is no growth there. Get ready for your next level.

Esther 2:9 "Before a young woman's turn came to go in to the King, Esther had to complete twelve months of beauty treatments prescribed for the women, six months with oil of myrrh and six with perfumes and cosmetics."

EAGLES FIND A PLACE OF RENEWAL

As they grow old, they go through a painful process of transformation. The eagle knocks his old beak on a rock to remove it. Once a new one grows it plucks its old feathers from its chests and wings and lives for another 30 years. Ladies, read books that will transform you. Watch things that will challenge and build you.

Romans 12:2 "Do not conform to the pattern of this world, but be transformed by the renewing of your mind. Then you will be able to test and approve what God's will is---his good, pleasing and perfect will."

An Eagle does not fight a snake on the ground, it picks it up high into the air, thereby changing the fighting ground, then releases it back to the ground. A snake has no stamina, no power, no balance in the air. It is useless, weak and vulnerable unlike on the ground where it is deadly, wise and powerful.

So, as a child of God, take your fight to the spiritual realm where God takes charge. Don't fight your battles or challenges in the physical realm; CHANGE THE GROUND LIKE AN EAGLE! You will be assured of a very clean uncontested victory. Pray and let God take control... the battle belongs to the Lord. Do not be quick to fight your own battles. Take them to God. He has promised to fight for you. Read Exodus 14:14 "The Lord shall fight for you, and ye shall hold your peace."

.

HOW TO PRAY FOR YOUR RELATIONSHIP/MARRIAGE

1. "Commit to someone who is prayerful," Love works best when both pillars are strong in prayer.

2. "Pray together," It is good to pray for your marriage/relationship, but when you pray with your spouse it is more powerful because you both are moved by one spirit towards one goal. There is strength in two.

3. "Pray with the right motive," If you pray out of selfish ambitions, or with a competitive attitude to prove you are more right than your spouse, or to manipulate your spouse your way; then you will be praying a miss.

4. "Be a worshiper," When you live a lifestyle of worship, prayer becomes natural. Play worship music more to set the mood of prayer.

5. "Communicate better," Talk to your spouse more. How will you know what to pray for if you don't know the issues in each other's life? Prayer ought to be specific.

6. "Treat your spouse well," Don't expect God to hear you when you are hurting your spouse or when you harbour unforgiveness and resentment. Make peace with your spouse, then approach God.

7. "Run to God first," When there is a problem or issue between you two, run to God first. Often many run to friends and family thus getting various voices speaking to the situation leading to confusion.

8. "Pray with Scripture," Back up your prayers with Scripture. God spoke through His Word and His Word will not return to Him void. God honours His Word. This way your prayers are made in line with God's will.

9. "Pray consistently," Prayer should be a lifestyle, not something you do once in a while or when problems come. Your love needs constant protection, direction, nurturing and improvement.

10. "Pray preventive prayers," Don't wait for problems to come then start praying, pray so that problems don't come. There are common areas in a relationship/marriage that have the potential of causing problems; those are pride, unfaithfulness, in-laws, money, work, health, parenthood and selfishness. Pray for these areas so that you navigate love well.

11. "Listen to God," Don't just approach God with requests, hear from God too. Sometimes a couple can get so busy chanting prayers that they don't pick up the areas where God is rebuking them, they don't pick up the direction God is giving.

12. "Don't cancel your prayers," Once you've prayed over an issue, don't go back acting contrary to your prayers, don't confess how impossible what you prayed for is, don't confess

your spouse/partner will not change yet you were praying that he/she changes, don't go gossiping to your friends how messed up things are.

13. "Be the answer to your prayers," Sometimes the things we pray come when we become the change.

14. "Go to war," Sometimes the attacks in your marriage/relationship will not retreat by one prayer but by persistent spiritual warfare and complimenting actions. Don't give up praying over an issue, stay in the war room, stand up for your love

15. "Be thankful," As God keeps answering your prayers, as a couple, remember to thank Him. A thankful couple is a happy and blessed couple.

ALIGN YOURSELF AND YOUR MARRIAGE IN GOD'S WORD AND PLAN FOR YOUR LIFE

Remember ONE WORD FROM God will change your marriage forever: Dr. Jennifer's favourite nuggets

COMMUNICATION IS A FUNDAMENTAL KEY TO SUCCESSFUL MARRIAGE. Talk to each other. Discuss and God will bring the solutions your way. Work it out.

SET DATE NIGHTS AND KEEP THEM. TO spend some time alone together is very important

NEVER TAKE YOUR SPOUSE FOR GRANTED. Treat your spouse with respect and love. Don't make demands but make requests.

UNDERSTANDING YOUR SPOUSE'S LOVE LANGUAGE. This will improve your marriage. Speak that language and you will grow stronger together.

TAKE RESPONSIBILITY FOR YOUR ACTIONS. Be responsible for your actions and be proactive in your marriage. Blaming or pointing fingers never solves anything. This strengthens relationships and trust.

Proverbs 14:1 Every wise woman buildeth her house

As a Wife, Your BEAUTY attracts your husband, but your WISDOM will continue to keep him! Your ELEGANCE catches his ATTENTION, but your INTELLIGENCE convinces him! NAGGING irritates your husband, but your "Constructive Silence" weakens him!

Remember that the "boyish" character in your husband comes out occasionally, but your ability to always handle it, is a sign that you are a MATURED WIFE!

Every man has "Secret Struggles and Pains, including your husband, if you should ever find them out from him, please exhibit the greatest maturity by asking the Originator of your marriage, (God) to help you with USEFUL IDEAS, that you will suggest to him (your husband)!

In the long-run, your WORDS matters to your husband than your "LOOKS"! So always invest the RIGHT WORDS! Earn your husband's respect and he will consider you as the yard-stick for all his actions!

Learn to mould your husband's moods, and he will naturally give you his "FUTURE" as he recalls your maturity in the past issues! Note that, WOMEN are everywhere, but REAL

WIVES are scarce, let the QUEEN in you come alive, and your husband will always hold you in a very HIGH ESTEEM!

Words every Wife and Husband would love to hear from each other: Make sure you send at least 3-5 of this daily.

1. I am so proud of you honey.
2. You still take my breath away.
3. How was your day?
4. Wear something beautiful. I want to take you out tonight.
5. I'm so in love with you baby.
6. You are right!
7. I am thinking about you.
8. I miss you so much.
9. I trust & believe in you.
10. Everything will be okay, we have each other.
11. I am Sorry, please forgive me.
12. You are the best.
13. You are great in bed.
14. You are my best friend.
15. I'm faithful to only you.
16. I'm praying for you honey. It shall be well with you.
17. After all these years. You're still the one.
18. In good times and in bad times...I will always be here for you.
19. Shhh Just Let me hold you baby.

20. You are so beautiful/ so handsome.
21. Come here sexy, I want you....now!!!
22. Can't wait to get home to you and our kids.
23. Put your feet up this weekend...I will do the chores.
24. I cherish our love; you were reserved for just me &our family.
25. Nobody out there will ever measure up to you.
26. You make me incredibly happy.
27. Our children have such a great role model in you honey.
28. I love your mind; your Intelligence is sexy.
29. Don't worry about that, I've handled it my darling.
30. You always know how to make me smile.
31. I have so much respect for you darling.
32. You are a great dad/ mom to our children.
33. Thank you for listening to me and caring about how I feel.
34. You are so good to me / balancing work with fun
35. You make this home beautiful and warm just by being there
36. You are God's most perfect creation.
37. Thank you for being a great provider.
38. I am your biggest cheerleader.
39. You have my support the blue print for our happiness
40. God blessed me when he blessed me with you.

Don't forget to Send at least five texts today and wait for the amazing expression from your husband's response. Amen

MAKE AN EFFORT TO GO FOR A HONEY MOON MONTHLY.

"Take me away with you—let us hurry!" (Song of Songs 1:4)

Is it time for you to take a romantic trip? Even if finances are tight, just being together can rekindle "that loving' feeling." All that is needed is a little effort and creative flair. Talk with your spouse, ask him or her what would bring new interest and excitement to your marriage. Then schedule at least two "getaway" activities a month when you can be alone together. If you keep the fire of your relationship well-tended with romance, you'll enjoy its warmth throughout your marriage.

- Have awesome conversations at the breakfast table.
- Be relaxed in front of the fire and just talk for hours.
- Plan a candlelit dinner somewhere for the evening.
- Begin to treasure those romantic moments from early days together.
- Send him a love note hidden in a Coke bottle.
- GO FOR DINNER
- GO FOR MOVIES
- GO FOR SPECIAL SPA
- GO FOR A DRIVE DATE, etc.

WISDOM FOR MARRIED LADIES ON VALENTINES DAY

SET UP CANDLES
Buy as many candles as you can for your Valentine's favourite scent. Arrange them in a pattern that will make him swoon. You can set them up so that they make a heart shape, or so that they look like your initials. You can even make them into an arrow that points to a room where you're waiting for him. Make Tokyo journey unforgettable.

PREPARE HIS FAVOURITE HOME COOKED MEAL
Men have two stomachs...I'm convinced. Why not surprise your valentine with a delicious home cooked meal this year? Also, you can take him out if that is what you choose. But let him know you are the best chef.

DRESS UP, FLIRT, FRENCH LOVE KISSES
Dress up and show off your flirty side this Valentine's Day with some of the most romantic surprises for your valentine! The amazing styles for kissing, actions will give you some really creative ideas to show him how much you really care! Through these romantic surprises for your valentine, both of you will fall in love more and deeper with each other, and you will both share wonderful times together! Enjoy each other as much as possible!
Today is your day of LOVE.

• Ask your husband to sing a love song for you or you could sing for him.
• Dance in front of your husband.

FINALLY, GET ONE BIG HEART SHAPED COOKIE ON A FLAT PLATE AND BRING TO HIS FACE AND SAY THIS ROMANTICALLY " Honey follow me and come eat my cookie " .... Leading him to the bedroom where Song of Solomon 7 will manifest live.

Song of Songs 7:8-12 KJV

[8] I said, I will go up to the palm tree, I will take hold of the boughs thereof: now also thy breasts shall be as clusters of the vine, and the smell of thy nose like apples; [9] And the roof of thy mouth like the best wine for my beloved, that goeth down sweetly, causing the lips of those that are asleep to speak. [10] I am my beloved's, and his desire is toward me. [11] Come, my beloved, let us go forth into the field; let us lodge in the villages. [12] Let us get up early to the vineyards; let us see if the vine flourish, whether the tender grape appear, and the pomegranates bud forth: there will I give thee my loves.

Tips for single ladies
Have Faith
Don't miss church events at all costs.
Get connected online.

I understand that Valentine's Day can be challenging for the single ladies, because you will be seeing married couples buying things and doing things for each other, and expressing their love for each other. And you will be thinking "I wish I had some to show love and be loved. But do not worry about too many things—YOU ARE NOT LEFT BEHIND. YOUR DAY IS COMING TO GET MARRIED IN GOD'S GOOD TIMING.

Don't let what the TV displays in your eyes be your nightmare, but begin to celebrate you.

CELEBRATE YOURSELF! LOVE YOURSELF TO THE MAX, AND TREAT YOURSELF!!!

On Valentine's Day go to a hotel and ASK FOR A TABLE FOR TWO; one chair for you, and the other one for the Holy Spirit. Don't stay home feeling sorry for yourself.

Remember GOD'S timing is the best than when you push and get hurt like we spoke earlier.

WHAT YOU CAN DO

During Valentine's Day do extra ordinaries just for yourself.

1. GO TO CHURCH AND PRAY. Go to the house of God if possible. On Valentine Day go and give thanks to God for he has been good to you that you are alive and well.

2. SPOIL YOURSELF
Make Valentine's Day a day to spoil yourself. Buy yourself chocolate, order pizza, eat ice cream, and rent your favourite movie. Just relax and be happy. Enjoy!

3. CELEBRATE YOURSELF: Go to a concert, do something spontaneous with your single friends. Have a Singles' Party where everyone can cheer and enjoy their single-hood. Girls Talk is always available for you.

4. BUY YOURSELF A GIFT. That Purse, Shoes you desired so much had eyes on it, go buy them. The book you saved in your Amazon account, or that video game that you dream of playing, now is the time to buy it. You will be so busy being excited by your new purchases that you won't even notice all the World's loneliness about Valentine's Day. You have something to celebrate for looking forward too as well.

5. GET YOURSELF A MAKE OVER
For example, you could get high quality products like HYBRD to use and feel good about yourself.
Change your hair Style, get a new haircut. Do your nails. Go to the spa. Pamper yourself. Make yourself better with

yourself. Go to the gym, run an extra mile. Read your favourite books and life-changing books like; The Power of Confession. Start on that home project that has been pending for some time. Whatever makes you feel rejuvenated go for it.

6. TIME TO RE EVALUATE YOUR VISION

Remind yourself why you are still single. Don't fall under the pressure or let someone tell you how to live your life.

If you're not ready for a relationship, that's your choice. There is so much exploration that a person should do before settling down. Why tie yourself down just for the norms of society? Think of your accomplishments and where you still need to go. Being in a relationship is time and commitment, and you should be able to enjoy it when you are ready for it, not when someone tells you. Plan to travel with our Girls Talk Mission trips around the world. We are now in 4 continents in 24 countries.

HAVE FAITH AND GET OUT THERE!

Please singles, make no misconception about waiting on God and having faith by all means, GET OUT THERE!

Ladies if you want to be found, get out there to be seen. Don't put God in a box and think that the only way you will get a husband is by staying and praying in the house or at church. Instead pray and get out of the house! Go to events with your sisters in the Lord. Go more places than just church and work. Find out what local events are going on and go with a good friend or two. It's certainly not a sin to getting out there.

Men do not ONLY look for a wife at church or work. Stop limiting God on what He can do and go beyond the norm sometimes. We are not saying do what is sin, do what corresponds with God's word.

Even if you pray for a husband there is NO WAY you are going to find one until you go outside of your job and church to find her, although many other couples have met that way. Go to single mixers, movies with friends, different church functions, local charity events, sporting events and more. Now I'm not saying you go to these places JUST to look for a husband, I'm saying while you are in these places you should be definitely looking! And it's true; sometimes you should go to these places in hopes of finding your king.

And one last thing for ladies: DON'T LET ANYONE make you feel desperate just because you want to be married. Single ladies seem to get this mostly after a simple expression they would like to get married, they are "desperate" or "not waiting on God". It's ok to speak the truth of your heart! It's ok to let a guy know you are not interested in casual dating but that you would like a husband. If it scares him away, GOOD! Because that means he's not your husband!
Go for drives to stores, malls, book stores and parks just to make yourself SEEN! Don't be in a hurry nor desperate to marry, but put your faith to work by being "findable"

So single ladies, don't be afraid to be upfront about wanting to be married, because it will SURELY get rid of the game players when you make it known you are about serving God and finding a mate!

Don't just have faith and stay in the house, but be wise in everything of course. GET OUT THERE!

James 2:17, "In the same way, faith by itself, if it is not accompanied by action, is dead".

James 2:26, "Just as the body without the spirit is dead, so also faith without works is dead".

S. E. R. V. E

Here are five rules for serving your spouse. You can remember them by the acronym **SERVE**:

S: **Supply what your spouse needs in spite of what you need, want or understand.** In counselling couples over the years, unmet needs are one of the major issues I've encountered. One spouse tells the other what he or she needs, but the other refuses to acknowledge that need.

Men and women are completely different and have different needs. When we ask our spouse to meet a certain need, we want him or her to listen first, then strive to meet that need—whether it makes sense to them or not. What they are saying is, "I can't do this myself. I need you to supply it for me." In other words, it doesn't matter what you want or understand. It matters what your spouse wants.

E: **Enjoy serving your spouse and do it with a joyful attitude.** Let's say you approach your spouse and say, "Honey, I need this from you." And then they roll their eyes or make fun of you. Or they just ignore you. When any of these things happen, the spouse with a need feels rejected.

The first reason God created us is to serve Him, but the second reason He created us is for marriage. That is our purpose, which means your husband or wife should never feel like a burden to you. You serve them happily and gratefully. That is the vow you made.

R: **Reject scorekeeping. Instead, serve with a spirit of grace and faith**. In the past, I've taught about serving your spouse and heard afterward from people who say, "Well, my spouse is bad. They don't deserve it. If I serve them, it will just encourage their selfish behaviour. They need to repent first."

I understand that thinking, but if we are following the example of Jesus, we have to remember that He loved us while we were yet sinners. He loves whether we deserve it or not. That's grace. If your husband or wife is doing the wrong thing, your best approach is still to do the right thing. This is called redemptive love. It means giving even when you don't want to give, and trusting God to use your sacrificial love to redeem your spouse.

V: **Vigilantly protect the priority of your marriage.** Marriage is so important that it has to be given priority in your life. In many of today's marriages, people are just too tired to meet each other's needs. They serve customers or clients at work. They serve their children when they get home. And then they are too tired to serve each other. God created marriage so that the marriage comes first. We should tell each other, "You come first. You get the first and best of my energies." That's God's plan and we have to protect it with careful attention.

E: **Expect to be blessed. Remember Jesus' promise?** "He who is greatest among you shall be your servant." He says that, if we humble ourselves and serve, we will be exalted.

We have to trust that He will honour and bless us for following His example of sacrificial, redemptive love. Marriage can be a challenge, but it always works best when a husband and wife are committed to serving one another. The strongest marriages begin with two servants in love. If you want to change your marriage, make the decision today to start serving your spouse—then trust God for the results.

The only way marriage works is if you serve each other. That's how God designed it. There are two reasons this is true. First, we can't meet our own needs. If we could, we wouldn't be seeking a partner in the first place. A husband has what his wife needs. A wife has what her husband needs. The best way to receive these things if we serve each other. Second, we swore allegiance to each other when we got married. We promised faithfulness, saying, "You're my source. I'm not going to go to someone else to get my needs met. You're the person who's going to meet my needs." Marriage requires a Christ-like love, which means we should love each other with the character of Jesus. Jesus is humble. Jesus sacrificed for us. Jesus came to serve. He said, "But he who is greatest among you shall be your servant" (Matthew 23:11).

I am convinced that marriage has become broken in the world because we are not Christ-like people. We are arrogant and self-absorbed. We don't like to serve. When you don't serve one another, your marriage falls apart. But if you're willing to serve your spouse, your marriage can thrive.

23 THINGS TO MAKE YOUR HUSBAND CLOSER TO YOU

1. Call him by a pet name.

2. Allow him to exercise his authority as the head of the family.

3. DO NOT challenge him when he is hurt.

4. Be silent when he is angry. You can go back to him in his sober moment with apology and explain why you behave that way that annoyed him.

5. Be quick to say "I'm sorry dear" whenever you offend him, insist on his forgiveness appreciate and kiss him when he does.

6. Speak good of him before his friends and siblings.

7. Honour his mother.

8. Insist that he buys gift for his parents and so be sure that he will do the same for your parents

9. Surprise him with his favourite dish especially when he has no money at hand and never delay his food.

10. Do not allow the maid to serve him food when you are at home, because you may lose him to her.

11. Give him a warm reception with an embrace when he returns, collect his luggage and help undress him.

12. Smile when you look at him and give him occasional pecks when you are out socially.

13. Praise him before your children sometimes.

14. Wash his back while he is in the tub or shower.

15. Put love note in his lunch box or briefcase.

16. Phone and tell him that you miss him.

17. Dial his number and on hearing "hello" just tell him I love you.

18. If he is a public figure or a politician, gently wake him at the early hours of the morning and romance him to the point of demand. He will not be enticed by any other woman that day.

19. Tell him how lucky you are to have him as your husband.

20. Give him a hug for no reason.

21. Appreciate God for the Adam of your life.

22. Always remember to pray for him.

23. Pray together and also pray together before going to bed in the evening...

May God bless your marriages.

Proverbs 18:22
Whoso findeth a wife findeth a good thing, and obtaineth favour of the Lord.

1. MISS "EXTREMELY JEALOUS"

If we're talking about types of women that men do not want to marry, we must surely include this very popular type of lady. She is always very distrusting and suspicious and even though she might have been hurt in the past, this is not an excuse for behaving like this in all her relationships. So, that's why, most of the time, guys will break up with her because after all "no one can go through his life being prosecuted for somebody else's crimes."

2. MISS "BOSSY"

At first, a man might think that this trait is kind of cute, that he likes a woman who is ambitious and knows what she wants, but after a while, he will realise that things are a bit different and he will "feel like he is in grammar school being told what to do by his second-grade teacher." So, if you recognise yourself in my description, try to do something about it and be more approachable.

3. MISS "PLAYING GAMES"

I know that sometimes, it may seem fun to play all sorts of fun games (well, fun for you), but in the long term this behaviour will surely damage your relationship. Maybe at first, a man will be intrigued by a hard-to-get lady, but after a while he will want to be with someone who is a bit nicer and more stable. So, no matter how tempting it may seem, stop playing games with his heart! Act a little bit more responsibly and think about his feelings too!

4. MISS "I HAVE NOTHING ELSE GOING ON

Men love a woman who knows what she wants, who makes plans that don't necessarily involve him, who has a goal in her life and who doesn't live only for him and for seeing him happy. So, ladies, no matter how in love you might be, don't forget about yourself or about your dreams!

5. MISS "DADDY ISSUES"

Experts said that this type of woman usually dates older and powerful men because deep down, she is actually looking for a father figure and not a partner whom she will want to marry someday. Maybe at first a man will be impressed that a younger woman finds him attractive, but after a while, he will realize that his special lady has a couple of issues that she needs to resolve if she wants to settle down with him.

6. MISS "I NEVER EAT"

This is another very frequent mistake most women make nowadays because they want to look good for their men: they never eat. It's not a healthy behaviour and in the long term, it might even have some serious consequences and you could develop an eating disorder. Also, keep in mind that a man loves you for more than the way you look and he will want to share his life with someone who appreciates the little things in life, like the joy of eating a cupcake while watching your favourite movie. You know, it's not fun to always eat alone.

7. MISS "I WANT TO CHANGE YOU"

This is another common mistake most women are tempted to do and it is trying to change their partner to suit their needs or wishes. Well, maybe that will work for a while and maybe some guys will even like that and will let themselves be changed because of their own insecurities, but keep in mind, ladies, most men find this type of woman quite unattractive. They wouldn't want to stay in a relationship with her for too long.

8. MISS "LOVES TO GOSSIP"

No wonder guys don't like this woman! This type of lady likes to gossip a lot and she enjoys talking about other people and other people's problems all day long. As a result, a lot of men will tend to act prudently around her because they never know what she might say about them behind their backs. Maybe at first, they will find her entertaining, but once they get to know her better, the only thing they will want to do is leave.

9. MISS "KEEPING UP WITH EVERYBODY ELSE"

Most guys will tend to avoid this type of woman because she is constantly concerned about keeping up with everybody else. She desperately needs to know that she is at least as good, as beautiful, as smart or even as wealthy as everyone she knows. Her behaviour and her dysfunctional beliefs can put a lot of pressure on her partner, who eventually will get fed up that she doesn't appreciate who she is or what she has and instead she wishes to be somebody else.

10. MISS "ATTENTION SEEKER"

I think we all know a girl who craves attention wherever she goes and just can't stand not having all eyes on her. She'll do just about anything to get people to look at her whether it's by her actions, her appearance or both. It can be fun hanging out with the girl who loves and commands attention, but being with someone who constantly needs to be in the spotlight can get old.

11. MISS "FLIRT"

This type of woman is similar to the attention seeker however, her main goal is to make her partner jealous. You can typically find her flirting with random dudes or showing off her assets. All of her actions are flirtatious in nature and loves any and all attention from men. Men like to be with someone who takes pride in their appearance, but no one wants to feel like they are constantly having to fight off other men because their girl is giving off mixed signals!

12. MISS "HIGH MAINTENANCE"

While there are some men who like high maintenance women, many won't dare marry someone who needs to be waited on hand and foot. We all like to be spoiled by our partner, but someone who never cooks, cleans or does much of anything besides demand the very best of everything might have a hard time finding someone who wants to spend their life catering to their partner's needs.

13. MISS "CLINGY"

You know this girl. The girl who has to constantly call, text or be with her man or she's not happy. The girl who needs the world to know how much she loves her guy and can't seem to talk about anything else but him. The girl who has to know what her guy is doing at all times. It's nice to feel wanted and loved, but this type of behaviour can be off-putting. It's great to show someone you care, just don't smother them.

14. MISS "MOMMY DEAREST"

This one is a little controversial since there are men out there who like to be taken care of, but most men will be turned off by a woman who treats them like a child. When I say treating him like a child, I'm talking about fixing his hair, wiping his nose or cutting up his food and feeding him when you're out in public. Most men would be embarrassed by this behaviour and let's face it, he already has a mother, let him be!

15. MISS "PARTY GIRL"

Party girls are fun to hang out with. They're wild, free-spirited and always down to have fun. As much as guys like a girl who can party until the wee hours, it's not necessarily one of the qualities they look for in a wife. While it's fun to be with the life of the party when you're single, guys won't be too keen on marrying someone who sleeps all day and parties all night.

16. MISS " PREACHER "

No matter how much you know the Bible, and no matter how spiritual may be, no man wants a woman who shoves scriptures and religious quotes down his throat. I am not saying don't talk about the things of God together, but you have to know when and how. Men are born natural leaders, so when they see you being all miss preacher all the time, it's like putting him off.

17. MISS JUDGE

Let's be real ladies, for we can be awfully critical and judgmental towards the men in our lives – sometimes for no good reason. Whether He is too sensitive, works too hard, and especially where his past is concerned, do not judge your man. Men do not like a woman who is always judgemental.

18. MISS TEACHER

The man has had teachers pretty much all his life—ever since he started pre-school—plus his own mother. He doesn't need anyone else to come and be his teacher. At first the man might be attracted to you because you sounded educated, especially if he is highly educated himself. But please be slow to speak and quick to hear. Don't be a miss know-it-all!

19. MISS MARRIAGE COUNSELLOR

My dear sister, you are still single, therefore you are in no way qualified to give anyone marriage advice, let alone the man you are currently dating. Man cannot stand a woman who is always telling others couples what they ought to do and how they should conduct their relationships. They find this meddling behaviour embarrassing.

20. MISS NOTHING.

The man might find you attractive when he looks at you, but no matter how beautiful you are, once he finds out that you are this type of a woman, he will completely do a *one hundred and eighty* degree turn around. Men find such type of a woman tiring—even though you have nothing going on in your life. You don't go to school, you don't work, there is no planning that you plan. Please do something!

TRAITS OF A GOOD WOMAN TO BRING HIM CLOSER

As a woman, the looks don't matter but you can possess some of these great traits inspired by Dr. Jennifer Proverbs 31:10

HONEST
No one wants to wonder if their partner is telling the truth. That's why honesty is so attractive. It reassures him that he's dealing with the real you, and not some fraud.

FRIENDLY
Men want you to become close with their friends and family. If you're friendly, then there won't be any reason for them to disapprove of you. That's why a friendly woman is an attractive woman.

FAITHFUL
Most men will leave you if you cheat on them. That's why loyalty is one of the most attractive traits that a woman could have. Men disguise a cheating lady like disease.

OPTIMISTIC
It's easy to be negative. Meanwhile, it's hard to be positive, which is why optimism is such an attractive quality.

MATURE

Immaturity is a major turn-off. No one wants to date a child. They want to date a responsible, adult woman.

CONFIDENCE
If you walk around the room with your shoulders hunched, you won't look your best. But if you stand tall and act like you're hot, everyone will start to believe that you're hot.

CLEANLINESS
A groomed lady is very attractive. If your hair is clean and nails are trimmed, then men are going to find you way more attractive than a model who stinks.

GENEROUS
He doesn't want to be in a relationship with someone selfish. He wants someone who will stick their neck out for him. That's why generosity is actually sexy.
Be funny. We're not the only ones who value comedy. A woman who can make him laugh is the best type of woman there is.

ACTIVE
It's no secret that men like women who take care of themselves. If you eat right and exercise, he'll find you incredibly attractive.

PUNCTUAL
Men hate to be let down. If you're late on a date, he won't be happy, but if you show up on time, he'll subconsciously find you more attractive.

MOTIVATED

Despite what you may believe, most men want a woman with a job. It's attractive to see someone with a high position and a big pay check. Money talks.

RESPECTFUL
Men don't want to be talked down to any more than you do. That's why he'll find you attractive if you treat him like a king.

PASSIONATE
Men love hot sex and hot kisses. That's why they all want a passionate woman. Be sexy and passionate.

SINCERE
Men don't like liars. They want to be with a woman who is sincere. If you pretend to be someone you're not, it's a turnoff. But if you're always yourself, he'll love you for it

KEEP IT COOL
You shouldn't freak out every single time someone disappoints you. Or if a nail chips or a friend sends you an insulting text. If you keep your cool, even in difficult situations, you'll impress any man.

You don't have to look perfect in order to be considered sexy and right for marriage. Just be of these or more good character.

Married ladies, I know that you love your husband so much and you'd never choose to hurt his feelings. But sometimes you can hurt his feelings without even meaning to. It's usually a result of not understanding what's hurtful to him.

1. NOT HAVING FAITH IN HIM
This may be the thing that hurts his feelings the most. Your husband needs you to have faith in him and his abilities. When he feels you don't, it's very hurtful. Your confidence in him means everything. Even when you're having your doubts about him doing something, it's a good idea not to tell him that. Look at Serah our mother of faith. Abraham woke up and told her God said we move to where he will show us. Bible doesn't say she resisted or put him down. No.

2. WHEN YOU RELY ON SOMEONE ELSE'S EXPERTISE IS VERY INSULTING WHILE HE CAN HANDLE IT.
If you rely on someone else's expertise over your husband's that can hurt him. As a general rule, he wants to take the first crack at repairing something or figuring something out. If it's not something he can do, he'll tell you. To put it simply, he wants the chance to be your hero. Giving him that opportunity will make him very happy. Let him fix that broken chair for you. When he is fixing go sit

down and watch him and tell him how you appreciate him around the house because he is your "BOB THE BUILDER" (cartoon character)

3. QUESTIONING HIS ABILITY TO DO SOMETHING HURTS HIS PRIDE

Your husband wants you to think he can do anything. Your doubt in his abilities is hurtful. It's true that the things that hurt your feelings are very different than his and that makes it even harder to understand. If you're feeling unsure about these things, have a conversation with your hubby about them. It can be really eye-opening. See women are different from men. Ladies, stop asking tight questions as if you are giving your husband an interview.

4. YOUR BODY LANGUAGE CAN BE HURTFUL

Most husbands aren't as verbal about feelings as wives are. Therefore, they read a lot into how you're feeling through your body language. When you roll your eyes or shake your head, they take that personally. It can hurt their feelings.

5. HE HATES IT WHEN YOU GIVE HIM "THE LOOK"

If you have children then this is probably the same look you give your children when they're misbehaving. It's a look that clearly says you disapprove of what he's saying or doing. It can seem harmless to us as women but men don't feel that way. It's something they can actually be very hurt from. While you can't tiptoe around his feelings, it's good to avoid hurting them. Same when you want him to avoid doing things that are hurtful to you.

6. PUTTING HIS JOB OR INCOME DOWN DEEPLY HURTS HIM.

This is not a good idea. It's never good to insult his job or income. Men take a lot of pride in their work. This is true no matter what his job is. It's best to keep comments about his job to yourself. Besides, he could have a strong 5-year plan in mind or know that he has opportunities for advancement. Just pray and suggests more income jobs but NEVER put him down.

7. HE'S HURT WHEN YOU TEASE HIM IN FRONT OF HIS FRIENDS

Your hubby may never tell you but it may hurt his feelings when you tease him in front of his friends. He doesn't want to look inadequate in front of them and your teasing can make him feel that way. You know you aren't trying to be hurtful. You're probably just trying to be funny and entertaining. A good way to find out if this bothers him is to watch his face when you tease him in front of his friends or just ask him if it bothers him.

8. WHEN YOU CHEAT ON HIM THIS WILL CUT HIM VERY DEEPLY

Naturally men are affected the same way as women they just deal with it differently. With men since they don't deal with emotional baggage as most women, that he will probably carry the cheating thing around for a while, I do not doubt that it will affect his future relationships. It will affect his relationships to an extend he hates women

1 Corinthians 6:18-19

Flee fornication. Every sin that a man doeth is without the body; but he that committeth fornication sinneth against his own body. What? know ye not that your body is the temple of the Holy Ghost which is in you, which ye have of God, and ye are not your own?

Proverbs 21:19 "Better to live in a desert than with a quarrelsome and nagging wife."

Proverbs 25:24 "Better to live on a corner of the roof than share a house with a quarrelsome wife."

Here are some five very dangerous toxins of the tongue that women, wives must work to avoid. These are home breakers. They are enemies to you and your marriage. These same negatives words at the hearing of your children, many kids are misread to their destiny. Watch out!!!

1.SARCASTIC WORDS. Sarcastic Words: Comments like, "The lawn isn't going to mow itself," or "Do I look like your maid?" seem like no big deal on the surface, right? But sarcastic words are sometimes just symptoms of an underlying unmet expectation that has frustrated a woman for quite some time. They can be used as a cowardly way to "dig" at your husband ...poisoning slowly.

2. UNSUPPORTIVE WORDS. Unsupportive Words: Every husband wants to know that they have their wives in their corner cheering them on. When a spouse says things like, "That's a crazy idea," or "Do you really think you can do that?" ...what they may really be saying is "I don't believe in you," or "I'm not on your team." Now, that's not to say you

shouldn't tell your spouse when you think they have a truly bad idea. But, instead of saying, "That's the worst idea ever," you could say, "That's a great idea, but I feel like you would be better at this..." Supporting one another's aspirations is essential to a happy and productive marriage. We should be our hubby's #1 fan, not their biggest critic.

3. DISRESPECTFUL WORDS Disrespectful Words: Respect is not something that has to be earned. It should be given unconditionally in marriage. Disrespectful comments like, "Can't you find a real job?", "I don't care what you say; I'm going to do it anyway", and "You've really been putting on weight" are insulting, offensive, and can undermine a spouse's sense of worth.

4. COMPARING WORDS. When saying things like, "Jonathan would do that for his wife" or "Why can't you be more like Ken?" what you're really communicating is "You don't make the grade...you're not good enough" as a husband to me.

5. SELFISH WORDS. "I don't care how you feel, just get it done." "I want that new dress." "I need someone who really meets my needs." Spouses who care more about themselves than their spouses often start their sentences with "I." It's all about their wants and their needs, rather than their mates.

Ladies, do you have any or many of these dangerous toxins of the tongue being injected into your marriage? If so, here are several antidotes you can use to counteract their effects.

• Apologise to your husband for all the poisonous things you've said to them over the years. Healing can only begin when toxins are removed. And in the case of verbal toxins, relationships begin to mend when couples ask for forgiveness from each other.

• Be slow to speak. There's an old adage that states that you never regret what you never say. It's okay to be quiet, reserved, and thoughtful about what comes out of your mouth...especially when you are upset.

• Make a personal vow that toxic words will no longer come out of your mouth. Putting a post-it note by your bed or on your mirror can serve to remind you of your commitment. Give your husband the freedom to inform you when toxicity starts to stream from your tongue. James 1:19 "Wherefore, my beloved brethren, let every man be swift to hear, slow to speak, slow to wrath:"

Just as Adam and Eve were naked and unashamed in the Garden of Eden—until sin entered their lives—true intimacy is only possible in an atmosphere of purity. For many marriages, unforgiveness is the sin that introduces impurity to the relationship. Maybe there's something in your spouse's life that you have not forgiven. A past hurt or offence may be affecting your ability to love each other as you should. That issue can be resolved with forgiveness. You won't know real intimacy in your marriage until you deal with it.

The Bible says unforgiveness poisons our hearts (see Hebrews 12:15). In marriage, unforgiveness is like a dead skunk in a basement: It makes the entire house stink. If you've ever been around unforgiving people, you've heard them speak venomous words about the people they resent.
But you don't have to hear their words to know what's in their heart. You can see it on their faces and in their actions. The venom of unforgiveness damages the vessel it is stored in worse than it hurts anyone you can spit it on. In other words, when you do not forgive others, the person you hurt most is yourself.

Unforgiveness doesn't just poison an individual's heart. It also poisons a marriage, even if the unforgiven offence isn't related to the relationship.

Harbouring resentment or bitterness toward others in your life will still have a negative effect on your marriage. In so many marriages, I've seen one spouse become the outlet for anger and frustration unrelated to the marriage relationship. If unforgiveness is poison, then forgiveness is a purifying agent. When we forgive others—especially a husband or wife—we get rid of unhealthy thoughts and feelings. Forgiveness cleans out the house. It blesses a relationship. It even impacts whether or not God forgives you, according to what Jesus taught in Matthew 6. Forgiving other people is a serious issue with God and one of the requirements of a marriage that follows God's Law of Purity.

There are five important STEPS to forgiveness:

1. Release
Release the guilty person from your judgment. Do not keep replaying the offence in your mind. Do not dwell on your hurt feelings or pain. Let God be the judge and let it go.

2. Decide
Forgiveness is a decision. Make a decision to love the person who has offended you, then let your behaviour reflect that decision. In cases of abuse or destructive behaviour, of course, you might have to limit your exposure to certain people. But your spirit toward them should be loving—not hostile.

3. Bless
Pray for that person. Jesus taught us to bless those who curse us and pray for those who mistreat us (Luke 6:28). This is one of the most powerful ways to change negative feelings

toward a person. I've seen prayer transform deep resentment and hurt into love and compassion—even without the presence of an apology. This is the most important step to take in healing the hurts of your past. Though it may take days or weeks, God uses this posture of prayer to heal us. By the way, the refusal to bless or pray for a person is proof-positive that you aren't forgiving toward them.

4. Move On
Refuse to bring up the hurt in the future. When God forgives us, He removes our sins "as far as the east is from the west" (Psalm 103:12). He doesn't simply forgive; He forgets. Though we cannot erase hurts from our memories, we can make the decision not to dwell on past offences. This decision alone can have enormous positive impact on a marriage.

5. Repeat
Forgiveness is often a process, so repeat these steps as many times as necessary. Keep going through these steps until you sense a genuine release of the unforgiveness in your heart.

A successful marriage is one-hundred percent possible if we follow God's laws for marriage. A marriage that obeys the Law of Purity must be one in which forgiveness is present. As you walk in forgiveness, you'll see a marked difference in the atmosphere and pleasure of your relationship. Purity is the environment where love and intimacy find their deepest and most beautiful expression. Forgive your spouse. Forgive those who hurt you. Be diligent to remain pure, and God will bless you beyond your wildest dreams.

SINGLE LADIES: RUN AWAY FROM UNAVAILABLE MEN

Job 24:15
The eye also of the adulterer waiteth for the twilight, saying, no eye shall see me: and disguiseth his face.

1. He drops you off and drives back to his wife and kids.

2. He throws away used Condoms as he goes home.

3. He buys sweets to clean your fragrance no matter how expensive it can be.

4. He forgives himself for cheating as he is driving to the mother of his Children.

4 He first takes shower to remove your unwanted sweats.

5. He then convinces himself that he can't leave his Wife and Children because of you.

6. He hugs her and ask his children about education.

7. He eats food cooked by his wife not two pieces of KFC he bought for you.

8. After eating he relax on the couch, and they both go to the bedroom.

9. They discuss about the future while she is lying on his chest.

10. Then they make love (Not sex which he had with you).

11. He doesn't take bath after it because he is used to that Aroma of his Wife.

12. She continues lying on his chest while discussing their investment, policies and planning their Anniversary.

13. And you are alone struggling with sex because he just did a fast.

14. He gave you 100K and your mother is boasting that she has a disciplined daughter not knowing that you are slowly turning to the resting zone of a bored Husband of someone.

My daughter, my sister, my friend it is not too late, know your values and have goals. This type of man will never take you anywhere. He is a hypocrite and not a real husband and father.

May your God-sent husband find you (Proverbs 18:22)

Isaiah 34:16 "Look in the scroll of the Lord and read: None of these will be missing, not one will lack her mate. For it is his mouth that has given the order, and his Spirit will gather them together."

CLEAN AND RENEW YOUR MARRIAGE NOW!!

If you are reading this book and it so happens that it is Spring, then God has a great plan for your life. But whether you are in Spring, Summer, Autumn or Winter, it is time to Spring clean your marriage. Your marital relationship needs constant cleansing. Marriage can be neglected from regular maintenance. You need to give your marriage some special quality time and attention it needs.

There are eight ways to spring clean your marriage.

1. LET THE PAST BE THE PAST
Are you holding onto any kind of grudge or hard feelings against your husband? It's easy to do. When you spring clean your marriage, this should be the first thing to go. Purpose to let go of your anger and resentment against your husband for things that happened in the past. It's as much of a gift to you as it is to your hubby.

2. ASK YOUR HUSBAND WHAT'S IMPORTANT TO HIM
From time to time it's good to check in with him. Ask him how he feels about your relationship in marriage now. Ask him if he feels like his needs are getting met and what's important to him. It's good to get this insight. Another plus to this is that many times your hubby will ask you the same questions in return.

3. COMMIT TO KINDNESS

Many times, the person that we should treat the best doesn't receive that treatment. We fall into the trap of believing that they'll put up with our crabbiness because they love us. While that's usually true, it isn't a good practice. Make a commitment to treat your hubby with kindness. After all, they mean the most to you so they should receive your best.

4. MAKE AMENDS FOR PAST HURTS

Just like you should get rid of all the feelings of hurt you've been carrying from past arguments, your hubby should, too. While you can't control what they do and don't hold onto, you can help them to let go of their past hurts by following this tip. Ask them if there's anything you've done that he's still hurting over. If so, ask if there's anything you can do to help him move past that. Many times, the fact that you care enough to ask will help him to let go of whatever he's holding onto.

5. START NEW TRADITIONS

Spring is a great time to start new traditions in your relationship in marriage. If things have felt boring or stale for a while then this is the perfect time to add in new traditions. Maybe you want to have more picnics at your favourite park or make it a goal to vacation seaside each summer. Talk to your husband and see what his input is on this. He may have some good ideas, too.

6. ADD EXCITEMENT TO DATE NIGHT

Date night doesn't have to be boring. Don't allow yourself to get sucked into the same old pattern of dinner and movie or whatever you do the most often. While dinner and a movie can be nice, don't be afraid to branch out. Try new things and enjoy new experiences together. You'll be amazed at the fun you'll have.

7. COUNT YOUR BLESSINGS

Many times, you can get too focused on the problems in your marriage. It's an easy enough trap to fall into. But it can have very negative consequences. It makes you feel sad and even hopeless about your relationship. Don't allow that to happen to you. Kick that attitude to the side and make it a goal to focus on all the positives in your marriage.

8. RENEW YOUR VOW BEFORE YOUR PASTOR

If you have been going through counselling with your pastor, it's refreshing to ask your pastor to renew your marriage vows again. It feels like new again and this time in the presence of God, The creator of all the universe.

DO NOT STEAL SOMEONE ELSE'S HUSBAND

WARNING AND PREVENTION OF PLAGUES:

CRIME OR SIN?
(It is not a crime, but it is a sin). IT IS SERIOUSLY NASTY TO STEAL SOMEONE'S HUSBAND OR FIANCÉ AS KARMA WILL BOUNCE-BACK ON YOU. Remember what you sow you will reap. Proverbs 22:8 "Whoever sows injustice reaps calamity,"

Galatians 6:7-8 "Be not deceived; God is not mocked: for whatsoever a man soweth, that shall he also reap. For he that soweth to his flesh shall of the flesh reap corruption."

1. IT'S JUST PLAIN MORALLY WRONG
DO NOT steal your friend's Fiancé or married man. This really shouldn't be something that needs to be taught! In a broader sense, homing your sights on a person or possession that is not yours is just a terrible attitude to have. Seriously consider your friendship before you act on any impulses. The years or special time spent forming a strong bond together. Take the high road and respect both your friend and yourself.

2 Peter 2:14-15 NIV "With eyes full of adultery, they never stop sinning; they seduce the unstable; they are experts in greed---an accursed brood! They have left the straight way and wandered off to follow the way of Balaam son of Bezer, who loved the wages of wickedness."

2. IT CAN AFFECT YOUR WIDER FRIENDSHIP CIRCLE

In a situation such as stealing a friend's fiancé or a married man, it is only natural that the members of your wider social circle are going to be forced to take sides in the matter. I hate to break it to you, but if you are the one who has done the stealing, you will quickly find that very few people will have any sympathy for you, and you run the risk of being completely ostracised by some of the people you love the most.

3. THE RELATIONSHIP WILL ALWAYS BE TAINTED

It would be fair to wager that most romantic attachments formed through the process of stealing a partner from a friend do not last as long as one would like or are as happy as one wants. The problem is that there will always be a cloud of stigma hanging over the relationship, including the thought that if your new boyfriend was so easily stolen, what makes you so sure he will not be stolen from you by another woman that catches his eye?

4. SO MUCH AWKWARDNESS!

It is very likely that you and your new boyfriend will have to completely change social circles as a result of your betrayal, change jobs, change church you love, change gym, change shopping malls, change address etc..., and in attempting to form new friendships with other people there will always be the awkward and lingering question of "how did you two meet?" Having to worry so much about such a seemingly innocent question is an indicator of all the awkwardness that may lie ahead.

5. THE GUILT CAN EAT YOU UP

If you have any shred of humanity, you will know full well that stealing your friend's fiancé or married man was the lowest of the low. It might have been too much to resist at the time, but the instant gratification of your newfound romance will soon be overtaken by a feeling of immense guilt for what you have done to your friend or his wife. The selfish nature of your actions will catch up with you and it can be a very unhealthy state of mind to be in.

6. YOU CANNOT TAKE YOUR LIFE BACK
Whether or not if your relationship with your stolen fiancé or married man lasts, one thing that will be forever is that fact that you cannot turn back the clock. Your whirlwind romance may burn out, but one certainty is that the friendships you ruin in the process of cheating will stay ruined forever. Even if you manage to achieve some level of forgiveness, your act of betrayal will always be in the back of everybody's minds.

7. YOU WILL GAIN A BAD REPUTATION
Gossip is a vicious activity even when the topic of conversation is something that isn't true; imagine what it would be like when people actually have a valid reason to talk about you? Even if this is your first indiscretion, thanks to gossip, the tag 'fiancé or married men stealer' will be with you in certain circles forever. Save yourself a lifetime of bad vibes and think before your act!

A MARRIED MAN IS AN UNAVAILABLE MAN

WISDOM FOR SINGLE LADIES

Single ladies, do not cheapen yourself by going after a married man. This is what happens when you date a married man:

YOU BECOME A SECOND-CLASS PERSON
The moment you agree to date a married man, you agree to be a second-class woman, and every second-class person is classified as a person of lower values.

YOU ARE NON-EXISTENT
Now look at it this way. If he is with you & his wife calls, he lies that he is still at the office or on an official assignment. You dare not interrupt his conversation or query him. But you can't call him when he is at home with family.

YOU BECOME HIS OWN PROSTITUTE
He sneaks you from his car into his hotel room but gives his wife his entire home.... My beloved sisters grow up, please!

YOU SELL YOUR FUTURE
He visits you at home & you introduce him to friends & neighbours as your boyfriend thereby blocking your chances of getting a genuine suitor, yet you don't even know the name of the street where he lives.... My sisters, how long will you continue to sacrifice your future?

YOU EVEN GET INVOLVED WITH UNBEARABLE

He takes you out & buys you assorted types of alcoholic drinks, yet he will never allow his wife taste even a drop of alcoholic drink. Common sense should tell you he is only doing that to get you drunk so he can truly destroy you in bed......My dear sisters, is your body good for experiment?

YOU GET PREGNANT BUT HIDE HIS NAME OR ABORT IT

He gets you pregnant & gives you money for abortion, but when his wife gets pregnant, he celebrates & gives her money for antenatal & baby things......My sisters remember he is already raising his family.

YOU ARE HIS HIDDEN STORY

Oh, just in case you don't know, he describes your emotions when he is with his friends but will never mention whatever happens between him & his wife. This makes all his friends see a lesser human in you.

YOU GET EXCITED OF LITTLE THINGS THAT DON'T MATTER

He gives you a few cash & you're happy not knowing that whatever money he gives you is what he calls "Body allowances"

YOU DON'T EXIST IN HIS PHONE

You have his picture on your phone & saved his number as "My Sweetheart" or whatever, yet your picture cannot be found on his phone & your number is saved on his phone either as generator mechanic or refuse dispose.......

PUT GREAT EFFORT, NOT EXPECTATIONS, IN YOUR MARRIAGE

Here are seven signs that tell you if you are expecting too much from your husband than you should:

1. WHEN YOU FEEL YOUR HUSBAND IS NOT GOOD ENOUGH FOR YOU

Do you often feel that your Husband is not good enough for you? Do you think you deserve more but you don't know exactly why you think this way? Apparently, your husband seems to be doing everything right but you still feel like your marriage is missing something. Well, have you ever considered that maybe you are just expecting too much from them? We are responsible for our own happiness, it's not somebody else's job to make us happy.

Genesis 26:1-2 "A severe famine now struck the land, as had happened before in Abraham's time. So Isaac moved to Gerar, where Abimelech, king of the Philistines, lived. The LORD appeared to Isaac and said, "Do not go down to Egypt, but do as I tell you.""

2. WHEN YOU ARE OBSESSED WITH YOUR HUSBAND'S FAULTS

If lately you seem to be focusing only on your husband's faults, on what they do wrong, and you tend to neglect all the wonderful things that they do for you on a daily basis, you should consider the possibility that you may be a bit too demanding. We all make mistakes and we all have flaws; nobody's perfect and neither are you.

Mark 11:25-26 "But when you are praying, first forgive anyone you are holding a grudge against, so that your Father in heaven will forgive your sins, too."

3. WHEN YOU HAVE HIGH EXPECTATIONS OF YOUR HUSBAND TO DO SOMETHING FOR YOU ONLY

We all want to feel loved and accepted for who we are with all our flaws and qualities, but sometimes, we tend to idealise our significant other. We expect them to be romantic, cute and funny all the time and no matter how busy or tired they are, they should always do everything in their power to make us happy. Well, we all have bad days, so try to give them a break every now and then, take some initiative and be the one who helps them feel better.

MY QUESTION IS, HAVE YOU PLANNED TO DO AMAZING UNEXPECTED THING TO HIM?
Luke 6:38 Give, and you will receive. Your gift will return to you in full-pressed down, shaken together to make room for more, running over, and poured into your lap. The amount you give will determine the amount you get back."

4. WHEN YOU EXPECT YOUR HUSBAND TO READ YOUR MIND

This is one of the most common mistakes that couples make; wives want their Husband to know exactly what they want, without telling them what that thing is. Especially in marriage duties and responsibilities they feel like their husband should understand them without having to explain themselves. Examples when you are in your monthly periods please communicate. Don't expect your husband to know. When you are feeling ill just communicate, please.

5. WHEN YOU WANT TO TURN HIM INTO A SENSITIVE HUSBAND

Do you often feel like you deserve a sensitive loving husband? Of course, we all want to be with someone who understands us, who cares for us, who makes sure that we are safe and who is very attentive all the time. Well, there's no such thing as the perfect husband. Instead, try to be the perfect wife yourself and see what effect this attitude will have on your significant other's behaviour. Don't ask sensitive questions like if a dress makes you look fat. And You know it and even you can see on your mirror. Men see and know they'll get in trouble if they don't give the right answer, so it's a stressful process.

6. WHEN YOU THINK YOUR HUSBAND IS LUCKY TO BE WITH YOU

I'm sure you are a great woman and that your hubby really is lucky to be with you but have you ever considered seeing things the other way around? Do you consider yourself lucky to be with someone as wonderful and caring as your significant other? Do you notice their qualities or all the amazing things that they are doing for you on a daily basis? Proverbs 18:22 "He who finds a wife finds what is good and receives favour from the Lord."

Ruth 4:14 "Then the women of the town said to Naomi, "Praise the LORD, who has now provided a redeemer for your family! May this child be famous in Israel."

7. WHEN YOU THINK ABOUT HIM NOT EFFICIENT OR THINK OF YOUR OWN FRUSTRATIONS, DO YOU CONTEMPLATE TO END YOUR MARRIAGE, GOD HATES DIVORCE!!

In Malachi 2:15-16 NLT Bible version says, "Didn't the LORD make you one with your wife? In body and spirit, you are his. And what does he want?

Godly children from your union. So guard your heart; remain loyal to the wife of your youth. "For I hate divorce!" says the LORD, the God of Israel. "To divorce your wife is to overwhelm her with cruelty," says the LORD of Heaven's Armies. "So guard your heart; do not be unfaithful to your wife."

This is very serious. The devil likes to confuse many marriages to completely disobey God's desire. Devil's mission is to destroy you and your God given vision.

When your partner frustrates you, do you often contemplate ending your marriage or starting a new one? When you are having a fight, do you always blame your husband for all the things that go wrong in your marriage? Try to re-evaluate your behaviour and see what are the things that you don't do right; because for a marriage to work, both of you should put in the effort and not only the expectations.

A lot of studies show that people's expectations influence their relationship satisfaction, so try to be objective and see if your expectations are reasonable.

GOD LOVES YOU AND CARES FOR YOUR MARRIAGE.

IT IS A STEP OF FAITH TO ACTIVATE YOUR BOAZ TO DISCOVER YOU VERY SOON. That way, you'll learn to find happiness without having to rely on another person. Even if you find a Potential Husband in the meantime, you'll still have a stronger relationship with him, because you won't always need him by your side.

"Now faith is the substance of things hoped for, the evidence of things not seen." (Hebrews 11:1 NKJV)

Here are a few of the best techniques for dating yourself before you date someone else

1. SERVE GOD WITH ALL YOUR HEART, ALL YOUR MIND, & ALL YOUR STRENGTH. God is your first priority; Eve had a good uninterrupted relationship with God before presented to Mr Adam. God looks when you get fully mature in this stage then he brings your BOAZ and introduce him to you.

2. LOVE AND TREAT YOURSELF: YES, GO OUT ALL BY YOURSELF. There are certain places that people consider "date spots," where they wouldn't dare to go alone. However, there's no reason for single people to avoid the places that couples frequent. You're allowed to go to the movie theatre alone or to a fancy restaurant alone. Sure, some people might judge you, but they aren't as secure as you are. You don't need a partner when you could have a grand old time all by yourself.

3. DRESS UP FOR YOURSELF.

Most people dress up to go out on dates. However, you don't have to wait for a guy to ask you out to wear something nice. You can buy a sexy dress, do your makeup, and then just lounge around the house. Of course, you should take advantage of the photo opportunities. If you're going to go through all the trouble of making yourself up, you might as well snap a few pictures.

4. BUY YOURSELF A TREAT.

Flowers and chocolates aren't reserved for women in relationships. You can buy yourself a beautiful vase of flowers to decorate your house with. You can buy buckets of chocolate to eat when you're bored. Don't be afraid to treat yourself.

5. LEAVE YOURSELF LOVE NOTES.

It's sweet for a husband or husband to be to leave notes around the car, fridge, door-house, but you can create your very own notes. Write yourself a letter to read whenever you're upset. Jot down compliments and stick them to your mirror. Put an inspirational background on your phone. Do whatever works.

6. MAKE A FANCY MEAL FOR YOURSELF

If you were in a relationship, you wouldn't go out to eat every single night. Once in a while, you'd make some fancy food. That's why you should create an elaborate meal for yourself, complete with candles. Then you can set a bath and enjoy your quiet night.

7. TAKE PHOTOS OF YOURSELF OR USE A PHOTOGRAPHER: LEARN WHAT MAKES YOU HAPPY

The point of dating yourself is to learn what makes you happy. Watch new games or movies to see what you like. Visit new places to see what interests you. Try to expand your knowledge of the world in order to expand your knowledge of yourself.

Signs that show he is in love with you:

"Then Naomi said, "Wait, my daughter, until you find out what happens. For the man will not rest until the matter is settled today." Ruth 3:18

1. He Treats You Well And Waits For Sex Until Marriage
A guy who loves you is considerate of your feelings, needs and desires. He makes them as important as his desires and needs. He is concerned with your well-being and will do things to make your life better, sometimes going out of his way to do so. Not only does he treat you well, he is also good to your family and friends. He respects your body and your wishes.

2. He Is Generous With His Time
He doesn't let too much time go by without seeing you. When he is available, he wants to be with you and chooses to spend his time with you. If you're in a long-distance relationship, he is spending time with you whenever your schedules allow. And you are together during major holidays such as Valentine's Day, Christmas and New Year's Eve.

3. He Makes You A Priority
You are at the forefront of his mind and he maintains contact in between the times you see each other. He considers you when making decisions and is considerate about doing things

you want to do. When speaking, he uses "we" instead of "I", and includes you in his future plans.

4. He Cares For You
A guy who loves you is genuinely happy for you when good things happen to you. He is compassionate when you're going through challenges. This guy is there for you in the good and not so good times. He thinks about you and surprises you with tokens of affection outside of your birthday, Christmas and Valentine's Day. He will also challenge you by calling you out on stuff to help you become a better person.

5. He Wants People To Know About You
He is affectionate with you in public by holding your hand, putting his arm around you and/or hugging you. He is proud to be with you and has introduced you to his family and friends. He brings you to family functions and get-togethers with friends, and takes you to company events.

6. He Treats Your Relationship With Integrity
He is trustworthy and loyal to you and your relationship. He is upfront with you about his past girlfriends and skeletons in his closet. He does what he says and will let you know if he's not able to. When issues come up, he is willing to work through them. Although he isn't perfect, he tries to be a better man.

7. He Wants The Best For You
A guy who loves you encourages you to do things you love, even if it means doing these things without him. He wants you to spend time with family and friends. He encourages you to find and live your passions, knowing that if you are

happy and engaged with life, you'll be happy and engaged in your relationship with him.

Ladies make sure you place less weight on his words and more weight on his behaviours and actions.

SIGNS HE MIGHT BE YOUR BOAZ

Some of you have been in various relationships that didn't work out. You thought he was the one but BOOM! He shocked and disappointed you. You were either blind, naive or refused to accept the truth when you saw the red flags waving. Sometimes we choose to write our love stories instead of allowing God to do his best .... you deserve the best. Don't ever doubt that.

Go through these signs and ask yourself whether you have noticed any of these:

1. **He's dating you with a vision:** He isn't in it for just fun and friendship. He desires to take it to the next level, and become your husband. A lot of men just string you along without a clear and proper vision for the two of you. A man with a vision will clearly define his intentions as soon as possible. He will not just be your friend or date you for a year without telling you his intention. If you've got time to waste, stay with him. If not, I advise you to move on. Habakkuk 2:2 days, "And the Lord answered me, and said, Write the vision, and make it plain upon tables, that he may run that readeth it."

2. **Check that your relationship must be exclusive:** Lately men are in the relationship game to date multiple women. Make up your mind that your answer is "No way". A sign that he might be your husband is revealed when you are his one and only. He won't share you or himself with anyone else. He'll prove that the norm that "all men are dogs", isn't

true. He's cut from a different cloth – husband material. When you are exclusive, he will give you all his attention and grow the relationship. Ephesians 5:25 "Husbands, love your wives, just as Christ loved the church and gave himself up for her."

3. **He believes in honesty in the relationship:** A great relationship is one which is very transparent and open. A potential husband doesn't care so much about your weight or make up. He believes you are beautiful and will only get better. His life is an open book and that will help you open up also. That is what friendship is all about – being confident in yourself.

Genesis 2:24-25 That is why a man leaves his father and mother and is united to his wife, and they become one flesh. Adam and his wife were both naked, and they felt no shame.

4. **You meet his family and he puts a ring on it:** For his family is vital key. It's been six months or maybe a year – have you met his close friends, parents, family and cousins? If not then don't see him as your husband just yet, he may be looking at another woman. You must meet the most important people in his life. That shows he's thinking long-term. The proof that a man wants to marry you is if he put that ring on it. Don't let him get away with just promising to marry you without proving it with a ring.

Esther 2:17 "And the king loved Esther above all the women, and she obtained grace and favour in his sight more than all the virgins; so that he set the royal crown upon her head, and made her queen instead of Vashti."

5. **He marries you with no intention of divorce:** Some men are addicted to just being engaged without ever being married! They were engaged before Jesus was crucified and

are still engaged after Easter Sunday 2014! Hahahaha! But seriously, what's the point of being engaged for so long? Maybe he got engaged to you so the pressure of getting married can be taken off. A man who wants to be your husband and wants you to be his wife will actually be more interested in setting a date for the wedding as soon as possible. Also, if he is a man who keeps his words, then he will keep his vows "until death do us part". His intention is to be married to you. Divorce is not an option.

Malachi 2:16 "For I hate divorce!" says the Lord, the God of Israel. "To divorce your wife is to overwhelm her with cruelty," says the Lord of Heaven's Armies. "So guard your heart; do not be unfaithful to your wife."

Have you noticed any sign that he is the one for you? What are those signs?

Your Next step is PRAYER: Begin to pray for your future marriage using one of my books *"The Power Of Confession."* Just like taking your medication, don't sleep until you pray and confess it daily. You will be building a firm foundation that will never be shaken. Despite of any storm, your marriage will overcome.

Next step is DELIVERANCE: Seek council from the wise about marriage deliverance. It helps because it's different from the former deliverances you went through before. This is deliverance from any generational curses to hinder you in marriage. And so on

The wife that wins all arguments with her husband is not wise. The home is not a law court.

The wife that uses sex as a weapon in the home – placing embargo, going to bed in jeans shorts and trousers – lacks wisdom.

The wife that uses the modern trends and laws of "women's rights" to insult or ridicule her husband simply makes a fool of herself

A woman that makes her home devoid of peace through bickering, nagging and quarrels needs help. A man should be eager to run away from office to be at home, for that should be the safest and cosiest place on earth for him.

Modern-day equality in marriage does not mean competition. It simply means partnership. Taking advantage of such equality to turn around and become the de facto head of the home and oppress the man is tantamount to playing with fire. If you destroy your home, soon you will be the boss of an empty home.

A wise wife makes the man feel so good that he assumes that he is the head. Once he gets that feeling, the woman gently wields her power and the head actually turns to wherever the neck wants without a protest.

A wife that does not pull herself away from friends' influence and advice or even from the control of her mother and father will have herself to blame.

When a man is looking for a wife, he bypasses women of different shapes and sizes to choose a wife. But soon after childbirth, many women hide under the excuse of childbirth to let go of themselves. Many stop bothering about their looks, shape, dressing, etc. Within 5 years of marriage, people start wondering if the wife is the man's aunt, even though she is 7 years younger. Her defence is that if he truly loves her, he should love her the way she is. But when looking for a wife, he saw people like the present YOU and ignored them and settled for the former YOU. Today, you go to bed smelling of onions and pap. You go to bed wearing grandmothers' clothes. Why are you playing with your marriage? Love is not about looks – we know. But looks enhance love and marriage. There is a difference between someone disfiguring herself and the person being disfigured by an accident. Please don't be complacent. As hard as it may be, work on looking like you were when he first saw you and began the chase.

If every night you are tired, sleepy, sore, down with headache or fever, "not in the mood," you are a joker, a serious comedian!

If your children suddenly become more important to you than your husband, you need prayers.

If you assume that as the woman, only you need to be pampered and fussed over while the man is a stone that has no emotions, you need to be pitied.

A woman that has the mind of a wife does not excite her husband. Wives are usually complacent and presumptuous. A wife must strive to have the mind of a girlfriend. A girlfriend is always nicer, sweeter, more loving and always thinking of ways to wow her sweetheart; a girlfriend does not try to win all arguments, does not call the man a "useless man", is not careless about her looks or dressing, always smiles and laughs with the man, sends the man sweet messages and calls, etc. Are you your husband's girlfriend in word and in deed?

When you rely on your beauty, cooking, character, connections and bedroom performance alone to keep your man and your home intact without putting God in the picture, you've missed it. Without GOD, it cannot be GOOD.

Put God first in your home, and keep Pride aside.

BE A WARRIOR

The warrior wife knows marriage is difficult, particularly if you don't put the time & effort into building a strong foundation. It gets easier with time, but during the process of growing into mature, selfless spouses, marriage requires A WILL TO FIGHT FOR THE UNION. Marriage is not for the weak-minded or soft-hearted. Marriage is for warriors. To be a Warrior-wife you must be willing to go to war for your marriage.

1. A PRAYER WARRIOR—a wife who knows the power of prayer. She intercedes for her husband & children. She doesn't wait for hard times to pray; she prays in good times & in bad times. When her husband needs prayer, he asks his wife because he knows she has a deep relationship with God. Her prayers soothe and comfort her family. They rebuke evil and cast out negativity. They declare goodness & favour in their lives. Not only does she pray, but she also believes what she prays. A POWERFUL WOMAN IS A PRAYING WOMAN

2. A WORSHIP WARRIOR—a wife who is not afraid to praise & worship God. She knows where her help comes from, & she expresses her gratefulness wherever & whenever the Spirit moves her. "Thank you, Lord," is her praise song.

3. A WORD WARRIOR—a wife who uses her words to speak life & wisdom to her husband & children. She knows how to encourage herself & her family in the Lord. Her words

heal, comfort & correct with love. On the other hand, she doesn't hesitate to speak in defence of her family when others try to harm them. She knows her tongue is a mighty weapon, so she uses it wisely.

4. A MOTHER WARRIOR—a wife who doesn't play when it comes to her children. She teaches them about God, about respect for themselves & about the importance of family. A mother-warrior believes her role as a mother is a divine responsibility & that God will hold her accountable for how she rears her children. As such, she does whatever it takes to make sure her children feel safe & loved; are fed & clothed; & are educated properly

5. A FINANCIAL WARRIOR—a wife who can take a few dollars & make a meal that tastes like a million bucks. She doesn't complain about what the family doesn't have; instead, she knows how to make do with what they do have. She plans for rainy days & helps her husband provide for the family.

6. A DISCERNMENT WARRIOR—a wife with a sixth sense to see & feel what's good & what's bad for the marriage. Because she prays regularly & hears from God, she can sense when someone has malicious intentions towards her family or when someone is a genuine friend.

7. A HOUSEHOLD WARRIOR—a wife who protects the peace & sanctity of the home. She doesn't allow negativity to infiltrate the home environment because she knows the home should be the safest place in the world for her family.

8. A SEXUAL WARRIOR—a wife who isn't afraid to enjoy physical intimacy with her husband. She initiates sex &

enjoys pleasing her husband. When the love life goes lacking or gets monotonous, she steps up to reenergise things.

9. A CONFIDENCE WARRIOR—a wife who makes her man feels like he can do anything he sets his mind to. She is a constant encourager who believes in her husband when he doesn't believe in himself.

10. A PURPOSE DRIVEN WARRIOR—a wife who knows that God has a purpose for her marriage. She's willing to fight for it when others say she should give up. She partners with her husband to achieve their marriage & family goals her motto is "Let's do this!"

I want to encourage you to embrace the warrior inside of you. As wives & future-wives, we don't have to accept whatever life throws at us. God made us in His image, which means we have the power to create the marriages & lives we deserve. Every woman has a warrior spirit on the inside of her. That's why "a man who finds a good wife finds treasure". Let's go warriors, victory is certain!
YEH!!! LET ME HEAR MY GIRLS TALK WARRIORS CLAIMING IT NOW!!
 "Am a Warrior in my family"
"Am a Warrior in my marriage"
"Am a Warrior in my business"

If you observe a lot of wives, you'll notice some differences. Some are really a great deal happier than others. While part of that depends on the type of marriage a wife has, although they're other factors. Let's talk about the habits that happy wives have that make a very noticeably huge difference in their happiness level.

Ephesians 5:33 "Nevertheless let every one of you in particular so love his wife even as himself; and the wife see that she reverences her husband."

1. MARRIAGE ISN'T THEIR IDENTITY

One of the first habits you'll notice about very happy wives is that marriage isn't their entire identity. While a happy wife loves her husband and treasures being part of a couple, she also knows she's still a unique individual. She doesn't lose herself in her marriage. While identifying yourself as only a part of a couple may seem like a good thing to do, it really isn't. The advice to take from this is to remember you're still your own person, even inside of a deeply committed relationship. Love you and accept you. Read 1 Peter 2:9

2. THEY RESPECT BOUNDARIES IN THEIR RELATIONSHIP

This one goes hand-in-hand with the first point. A wife that doesn't base her sole identity on marriage understands and respects boundaries between herself and her husband. She allows her husband to have room to make his own decisions as the head of the house. She's fully confident that her husband can handle his life. While she'll give advice if asked, she's comfortable giving him room to handle things on his own. Read Ephesians 5:22-23

3. THEY DON'T GET UPSET OVER GAMES NIGHT
They don't get upset over movie night, football, a golf or game or whatever it is that their husband does for fun. They give him space to do whatever he wishes to feel refreshed and refuelled. They realise he'll come home happier which is a plus for their marriage. Most happy wives have also learned to use this time to get their own fun thing going. Time for girls Spar with friends, church conferences. Read Proverbs 18:24 KJV, Proverbs 19:14

4. THEY AREN'T CLINGY
Happy wives aren't clingy wives. They're loving and affectionate but without crossing the line into being clingy. They're very comfortable giving their husband space. In return, their husbands are usually romantic and enjoy pursuing their wives. A bit of space can actually make a man become more romantic. Read Psalm 127:1

5. THEY TAKE CARE OF THEMSELVES
Happy wives take care of themselves. They don't feel the need to neglecting themselves in order to be part of a married couple. They know they can do both. A happy wife takes care of herself physically, mentally and socially. She makes time for things like working out, enjoying a favourite hobby and a night out with the girls. Read 1 Corinthians 6:19

6. THEY'RE CONFIDENT WOMEN
Lastly, happy wives are confident wives. They don't have a lot of insecurities. That's because they've dealt with those and realise their worth. They have confidence which their

husbands find incredibly sexy. Becoming confident is something each of us can do with some work within ourselves. Read Galatians 2:20

Just like a good driver takes his lovely car for MOT, so marriages need a check-up after every 6 months. In TKC our Archbishop always advises all married couples to book an appointment for their marriage MOT, either to receive counsel from ourselves or our church marriage Counsellors. Since I have been offering counselling service to many, I have found out that there are 7 TRUTHS AND GREAT HELP when you go as a couple for the couples MOT.

Have you ever considered this for your relationship? Many married people always neglect couples MOT service but those who choose to go for it, they actually normally benefit a lot. Huge help.

1. YOUR RELATIONSHIP DOESN'T HAVE TO BE IN TROUBLE IN ORDER TO GO FOR MOT THERAPY

Couples MOT is believed to bring out the best for their relationship and makes a good point after all. Couples MOT therapy is for anyone. Some people go because their relationship is on the rocks, but others go because they've hit a minor bump or for prevention of future problems occurring.

2. IT'S A SESSION WHERE YOU CAN BE REAL AND SHARE YOUR HEART

One beautiful thing about couples MOT therapy is that it's a place where you can be real with one another. The goal is to share your hearts and reach to an understanding. Sometimes you don't always do that in relationships. It's easy to hide your feelings because you're afraid of confrontation. You might be afraid of sharing your heart because you don't want to be that vulnerable. Couples MOT therapy makes it easier for both of those things to take place.

3. YOUR MOT THERAPIST CAN HELP YOU BY PLAYING AS YOUR MEDIATOR

Your MOT therapist is NOT your friend. They can help you navigate the rough waters of your relationship. It's almost as if they hold up a caution light to your marriage relationship when things get heated. They can help you redirect your conversations and find a common ground. One of the biggest parts of your therapist's job is to be your mediator. They pray, intercede for you and your marriage too.

4. YOU'LL LEARN SKILLS ON HOW TO COMMUNICATE IN A HEALTHY WAY

One of the best parts of couples MOT therapy is learning how to communicate in a healthy way. Your MOT therapist's goal is to teach you the skills you need so that your relationship can be at its best. Learning better ways to communicate is always a good idea. Many times, the problems that occur in relationships are from misunderstandings in communication. Learning to communicate better could practically eliminate that. Teaching you also when to listen and when to talk.

5. YOUR MOT THERAPIST CAN DIAGNOSE AND INDICATE PROBLEM AREAS IN YOUR RELATIONSHIP

You might be in a situation where the same issue keeps coming up. It never seems to be resolved. Your MOT therapist could be of great help here. They have the unique perspective of an outsider coupled with the knowledge of a professional. They deal with situations like yours every day so they can cut right to the heart of it.

6. EVERY COUPLE HAS DIFFERENT NEEDS FROM MOT THERAPY

Every couple is unique and all couple's issues are unique. You may not be going to MOT therapy for the same reason as the couple before you and that's okay. Concern yourself less with the reasons other people go to couple's MOT therapy and concentrate on your own relationship. Don't let MOT therapy make you feel like your relationship is doomed. Choose to view it as something healthy you're doing for the future of your relationship.

7. YOU COULD ACTUALLY END UP LOVING AND THANKFUL FOR YOUR MOT THERAPY

Couples MOT therapy could end up being the highlight of your week. It could be a time when you really connect with one another. It's true that some upsetting issues may have to be addressed, but that could help you emerge as a stronger couple. That's a goal that every couple wants to reach. Couples MOT therapy could be a wonderful thing for you. You leave better than you came in. You can even laugh at some of misunderstandings you had before. It's a refreshing and revival time.

The main reasons why couples would go for couple's MOT:

1.Sense of something missing/lost in the relationship
2.Lack of communication with spouse
3.Escalating arguments/ circular arguments
4.Loss of intimacy and sexual desire
5.Impact of professional life on the relationship
6.Adapting to marriage or becoming parents

I want you to know it is never God's plan and desire for a husband and wife to be having crises. Marital crises are a proof that something is wrong. Listen, in a family where there's constant crises the devil has gained ground to tamper with the future of the children.

Carefully follow the outlines below to help you manage your home effectively...

1. Mutual agreement: Let there be mutual agreement between you. There will be arguments and disagreements but learn to agree together to deal with whatever issue. Don't go to bed with unresolved arguments.

2. Service: You must admit with me that marriage is about service. How much can you serve? The husband must serve the wife and the wife must serve the husband. It takes understanding to achieve this.

3. Continuous cleaving: You must continue to cleave together. Stay together. Regular good sex and love making. How can you stay one week without having sex? Something is not well. When you stop cleaving the bonding will begin to break eventually.

4. Submission and accountability to authority: Who do you submit to? You must submit to God. You must have people

that can talk to you such as parents, pastors and spiritual leaders. Don't lose this relationship.

5. Spirituality: Don't let the devil break the spirituality of your home. What happened to the family altar? If toy can protect the altar, then devil can't come in.

Kisses are lovely. But hugs are fabulous too and I think sometimes we overlook their value. There are many times a hug can happen where a kiss can't, won't or shouldn't. And there are plenty of benefits to hugging too. Not convinced a hug is better than a kiss? Read on to be convinced.

SHOWS YOU CARE. A hug can act like a great big security blanket for its recipient, showing them that you care and that you are there for them.

LIFTS THE SPIRIT. When you hug or are hugged, something called oxytocin, also coined as the cuddle hormone, it released, and it makes us feel all soothed, warm and relaxed!

HELPS THE HEART. It has been scientifically proven that the act of a great hug can significantly lower a person's heart rate, which in turn can decrease their risk of several different heart related health problems!

ASSURANCE. There is nothing quite like the comfort and reassurance that a really good hug can give to a person. Something about the intimacy of body contact can be very relaxing and much needed.

GIVES OTHERS A SELF BOOST. The recipient of a hug can often feel a nice boost of self-esteem afterwards, and this is because of the voluntary closeness that they have just experienced with a loved one.

REDUCES LEVEL OF STRESS. It's a fact that a good, long hug can actually reduce the levels of cortisol in your body, and cortisol is the hormone that triggers amounts of stress.

Do you know THERE IS A NATIONAL HUG DAY National Hug Day is celebrated all over the world <u>on January 21st</u>, so get involved and become one of many huggers on that special day!

HUGS IMPROVES COMMUNICATIONS Regular hugging can improve your non-verbal communication with your loved one, as you start to pick up their body language much better

DIFFERENT SLEEPING POSITIONS

You should be aware of the comfiest ways to sleep in the same bed with your husband—for the sake of better sleep for both of you. Even though cuddling throughout the night seems like a great idea, it's far too easy to get uncomfortable and hot. Certain positions will make your arm fall asleep or your neck crick. If you want to get a good night's sleep, then you should use one of the comfiest ways to sleep in the same bed with your husband:

1. SPOONING. In order to spoon, both of you should rest on your sides, facing the same direction. Now let him place one arm around you and the other arm wherever he pleases. This is one of the comfiest ways to sleep in the same bed as your hubby, because it'll make you feel protected. His whole body will be pressed against yours, so you'll never forget that he's right there with you, waiting to kiss your lips.

2. ON HIS CHEST. If he decides to sleep on his back, you can rest your head on his chest. You've probably already done this on the couch while watching Tv together, so you should be used to the position. As long as he doesn't need the blankets reaching all the way up to his neck, you should both be comfy.

3. FACE TO FACE. You can rest on your sides, facing each other, so that you can open your eyes to see his cuteness. You can choose between keeping your hands at your sides, or

placing them on his body. You could even touch foreheads while you sleep to remind yourselves of how close you are.

4. HOLDING HANDS. Sometimes, you don't want to be on top of each other, because it'll cause your temperatures to rise. If you want to sleep on your back, separated from each other, then you can simply hold hands. It's a simple way to feel connected to him while you sleep.

5. REVERSE SPOONING. Traditionally, the man spoons the woman. Of course, the woman can be the one who spoons her man if she wishes. Press your chest against your hubby's back, and wrap an arm around his torso. That way, you can squeeze him whenever you'd like.

6. BACK-TO-BACK. If you're a fan of sleeping on your side, but don't want him snoring into your ear, you can sleep back-to-back. You're still touching, so you have a sign of contact, but you won't be causing each other any trouble.

7. MAN ON TOP. He might want to be the one to lay on your chest, so don't be afraid to switch things up. If he lays on you, it'll be easier to stroke his head and run your hands over his back. It's a sweet way to feel like you're helping him get a good night's sleep. You love him, so why wouldn't you want him to be as close as possible?
You don't have to remain in one sleeping position throughout the entire night. Plus, you're bound to shift in your sleep, so it's not something unusual for you to try out every single one of these cuddling moves in one night.

"Many waters cannot quench love; rivers cannot wash it away." Song of Songs 8:7

I PRAY FOR YOU; Our dear Heavenly Father, today I pray for all our Girls Talk Marriages that each and every couple will experience more love, better communication and deeper intimacy in their marriages. Lord, I thank You for the blessing of romantic attraction upon their marriage. May they and their spouse pursue each other joyfully and creatively all the days of their lives in Jesus' name. Amen.

No matter how hard we try to define this romance, it remains a mystery. Yet Solomon's Song of Songs does give us several clues to its nature:

• "My lover is mine and I am his" (Song of songs 2:16);

• "My heart began to pound for him" (Song of songs 5:4).

• "How beautiful you are, my darling!" (Song of songs 4:1).

• "All night long on my bed I looked for the one my heart loves; I looked for him but did not find him" (Song of songs 3:1).

• "He has taken me to the banquet hall, and his banner over me is love" (Song of songs 2:4).

• Come away, my beloved, and be like a gazelle or like a young stag on the spice-laden mountains. (Song of Songs 8:14)

• Let me hear your voice; for your voice is sweet, and your face is lovely. (Song of Songs 2:14)

OH, the book of Song of Songs reaches its climax with a description of the power of love, "Love is as strong as death, its jealousy unyielding as the grave. It burns like a blazing fire, like a mighty flame" (Song of songs 8:6).

BENEFITS OF EARLY MORNING SEX (FOR COUPLES ONLY)

They say having sex first thing in the morning not only improves your love life, it is also beneficial to your health. Early morning sex puts a smile on your face, boosts your health, looks and relationship. Scientists say people who start their days by having sex are all-around healthier and happier than those who don't.

Because it feels good, having sex in the morning makes you stronger and more beautiful. It releases the feel-good chemical oxytocin, which makes couples feel loving and bonded all day long and climaxing releases chemicals that boost levels of oestrogen, which improves the tone and texture of your skin and hair.

Some other benefits of morning sex include:

1. Apart from the fact that regular morning sex makes you feel upbeat for the rest of the day, it also helps in building a stronger immune system.

2. Believe it or not, it makes you less
susceptible to catching a cold or flu and can also improve the quality of your hair, skin, and nails.

3. Having morning sex three times a week
lessens the risk of a heart attack or stroke.

4. You aren't bothered by the responsibilities of the day yet and your mind is clearer.

5. You've just been sleeping and are hopefully well-rested and can devote more energy to sex.

6. Sex is relaxing and can help manage stress.

7. You start the day more in sync when you've pleasured one another both physically and emotionally.

8. You show your spouse that he/she is a priority, and so is your sex life.

9. Sex is exercise. It's a great way to work up an early morning appetite as breakfast is the most important meal of the day.

10. Early morning sex can be a great incentive to wake-up and put you in a more positive mood. Wake-up sex will help you feel happier and healthier throughout the day.

A MOTHER-IN-LAW

How to work your relationship with your mother in-law
Almost every comedy sitcom has them, at least 90% of our friends and co-workers are constantly complaining about them, and chances are you acquired your very own the day you married your man. Yes, I'm talking about meddling mothers-in-law. Perhaps one of the most powerful forces in the universe, and certainly one of the most frustrating, mothers-in-law often end up putting an incredible strain on our marriages. But, since there is little we can do to make them disappear, here is a list of 8 ways to handle a meddling mother-in-law. And no, murder is not one of them!

1. TALK TO YOUR PARTNER
While you cannot expect your husband to immediately pick up the phone and set his mother straight, he needs to know how she makes you feel. Without making him feel like he is stuck in the middle, ask him what he thinks the best thing would be for you to do. Perhaps he could mention to his mother that he does, in fact, like your cooking and that your hair is great just the way it is. She has to hear it directly from her son—that's the only way she will understand.

2. DON'T PASS ALL THE BLAME
While you may secretly wish that a house would fall on her, you also know deep down that your mother-in-law really does have her son's best interest at heart. Instead of simply placing blame all the time, make an effort to understand why she does the things she does. Take some time to consider

whether you may be partially to blame for some of her actions. Maybe slight adjustments on your part can make for a better relationship. More than likely she has no intentions of changing her ways, but if you can make little changes she will have that much less to complain about.

3. SIT DOWN AND TALK

Obviously getting your mother-in-law to hear what you have to say is not an easy task, but it may be all that it takes to make a friend out of your supposed worst enemy. The man you married is her little boy and always will be. Sit down and talk to her and help her to see that you love him just as much as she does but that love for your partner is completely different than love for a child. She might think that you do not adequately love her son because you show your love differently than she does—if you can make her see this, your life will be a whole lot easier.

4. KEEP HER INVOLVED

If you really think about it, the thing that most likely causes mothers-in-law to act the way they do is the fact that they feel like they are being replaced. The way you feel when she shows up for a weekend and takes over your house is how she feels every day. For years she has prided herself on taking care of her son and now some other woman has taken her place—it's a lot to deal with. Invite her to family gatherings, backyard barbecues, and even just for dinner. Making sure she knows she is still a part of your family and that her son and daughter-in-law want her around is all some mothers-in-law really want.

5. MAKE HER FEEL IMPORTANT

Let her know that she is still needed and important. Ask her to help with specific things at dinner, for example—like making her famous potatoes or baking her award-winning pie. Or ask for her help when you are planning a party or event; you may not ask because you don't want her to be inconvenienced, but she truly does want to feel needed and appreciated. Even things as simple as asking for her advice (even though it may be the last thing you want) will let her know that you value her opinion. Ask questions about your husband as a child, let her tell you stories, and tell her she should be proud of her son.

All of these little things let her know how important she really is.

1. GIVE IT TIME
If your mother-in-law doesn't like you, try to wait it out and see if the situation improves. An initially difficult relationship can evolve into one of mutual tolerance, and even friendship. It may take years for this change to occur, but it can happen, much to your surprise.

2. TRY TO MAKE FRIENDS
Try to cultivate a friendship with your mother-in-law. Even if you don't particularly like her, get to know her a bit better. You may have more in common than you think (and not just that you both love her son). Talk to her about her interests and thoughts, and she may start to see you in a more positive light.

3. UNDERSTAND HER
Is there a reason behind your mother-in-law's attitude towards you, however unfair it may be? Try to understand where she's coming from, and you may be able to improve your relationship with her. Mothers can feel threatened by the 'other woman' in their son's life and see her as a rival. Show

her that she is still an important person to him - and that she
could be to you.

4. TALK TO HER
Is your mother-in-law the kind of person who will discuss
difficult topics? If so, talk to her about your difficult
relationship and try to clear the air (without being
confrontational and blaming her for anything). Make it clear
that you want to have a good relationship with her.

5. NOTHING PERSONAL
Remember that her dislike of you is not a reflection on you
as a person; it's more likely a problem within her. Perhaps
she was very fond of her son's previous partner and isn't
adapting too well to his new relationship. And if you really
can't change her attitude, it doesn't mean that you're not a nice
person, or that the relationship is doomed to failure.

6. PARTNER'S SUPPORT
Enlist your partner's support and ask him to back you up if
his mother treats you badly. She should at least respect you
as the woman her son has chosen to be with, and he should
make it clear that he expects her to be civil. If he won't
support you, then perhaps the problem is between you and
him, not you and her ...

7. DISTANCE
If your mother-in-law really is unpleasant towards you, and
nothing you try can make any difference, the only option may
be to keep away from her. Your partner can still have a
relationship with her, and go to see her without you. There's
no point in spending time with someone who acts
unpleasantly to you.

BECOME CLOSER TO THE MOTHER-IN-LAW

Become a close friend with your mother-in-law even when she is difficult.
If you are looking for ways to bond with your mother-in-law, look no further. I can help you. There are things you can do to help the two of you form a relationship, no matter how difficult she may be. Try these ways to bond with your mother-in-law to revolutionise your relationship.

1. INVITE HER TO LUNCH
You know, one of the best ways to bond with your mother-in-law is to just bite the bullet and make the first move. Invite her to go out to lunch with you. Going to lunch is a little thing you can do that has a light-hearted manner about it. Yes, go out to lunch. It is a definite bonding invitation you can give her. Even if she declines, at least you have opened the door.

2. ASK HER TO TEACH YOU TO COOK YOUR HUBBY'S FAVOURITES
You know, next to you, this is the woman your husband loves best in all of the earth. It is really worth the effort to try to bond with her. No doubt there are things that your mother-in-law cooks that are favourites of your husbands. Ask her to teach you how to cook them. More than likely, she will be delighted to do so.

3. ASK HER ADVICE ON SOMETHING
If you have the kind of mother-in-law who loves to give her advice on everything, why not allow her to? I do not mean to

allow her to meddle in your business, but ask her advice about something. It allows her to air her opinion and feel important at the same time. It can also bring her closer to you because you opened up to her in this way.

4. GO SHOPPING TOGETHER

Shopping is a great way to bond with your mother-in-law. First of all, there isn't a lot of chatting because you are busy shopping. Secondly, it is fun and you can make a few fun memories while you are shopping. Thirdly, you are allowing her a window into your private world by letting her learn your tastes and preferences. You can learn some things about her, too.

5. TREAT HER TO A PEDICURE

Why not treat your mother-in-law to a pedicure? I don't know anyone who doesn't love having a pedicure done. While you are having your toenails painted, you will most likely both be relaxed and the tension between the two of you will drop significantly. A day out doing something that is meant to be bonding will hopefully have the desired effect. You may go home having gained a new friend.

6. SEND HER A CARD

Why not send your mother-in-law a card? You can use that as an opportunity to tell her that you know your husband is the wonderful man he is in part, because he was raised by her. It is true. She has a great bearing on his life and giving her credit for that is the kind thing to do. This means a lot to a mother's heart.

7. GIVE HER TIME

You know, there are just some mothers-in-law that are difficult cookies. A lot of these gestures will not help with them, although they will with most. If you have that particularly very difficult mother-in-law, you may just have to give her time. Continue being the beautiful, wonderful person that you are and hopefully she will eventually see that. Even if she never does, you will have the satisfaction of knowing that you did your best to be a good daughter-in-law to her.

HOW TO BOND WITH A MOTHER-IN-LAW

Bonding with a difficult mother-in-law can be, well, difficult. How have you overcome mother-in-law difficulties? I would really love to know.

If you're getting married soon, or if you've been married for a while, chances are, you might need a few tips for getting along with your mother-in-law. She's used to being the most important woman in her son's life, so the transition to the back burner might take a little getting used to. How can you make the change a little smoother, and keep your new family happy? Here are 7 tips for getting along with your mother-in-law.

1. LISTEN… OR AT LEAST PRETEND TO
She's going to have lots of advice, most of which you won't ask for, but one of the best tips for getting along with your mother-in-law is to listen to her, to give her your ear. Listen while she advises you on how to keep house (even though you already know how) and raise your kids (even though you already know how), and smile sweetly, even if you intend to ignore her advice. A little listening can go a long way. And who knows? She might just have some advice you can actually use!

2. ASK FOR RECIPES
This starts a little stretch of stuff you can ask your mother-in-law that will flatter her, and might just help your relationship over a rocky patch. Ask her for the recipe to that soup your

husband loves when he's sick, or the appetizer she brought to the family reunion last summer. She'll appreciate the gesture, even if she knows, deep in her heart, you'll never make it as good as she does.

3. ASK FOR PHOTOS
I know that, as a mother, I pride myself on being a font of embarrassing photos of each of my children. Chances are, your mother-in-law has a shoe-box or two, or a few albums, full of photos of your husband in that bad 1980s mullet, or the plaid "grunge" flannel from the 1990s, or (perhaps the best yet!) the naked in the tubby baby photos! Ask her for a few, and giggle with her over them. Bonding moment!

4. ASK FOR ADVICE!
That's right! Sometimes, one way to get closer to your mother-in-law is to ask her advice on topics you know she's actually able to help with. Is she a wine expert? Ask her to recommend a white for Thanksgiving dinner. Does she own the "laundry and stains" category? Ask her how to get that stain out of your husband's dress shirt. She'll be flattered that you want her help, and again, she might be an excellent resource!

5. DEFER BUT NOT TOO MUCH.
There's a fine line between forging a bond with your mother-in-law, and losing her respect for not being able to do anything to take care of her son and grandchildren on your own. Be respectful, ask advice, and defer, but not too much. You are, after all, the woman your husband chose, so she has to trust his judgment, and he has to back you, too.

6. ENCOURAGE HIM TO BE IN TOUCH

Nothing will irritate or hurt his mother more than if he disappears from her life once he marries you. Encourage your husband to be in touch with his mother, with at least a phone call once a week. Clear it with him first, but feel free to ask her out to dinner, so she doesn't feel like she's lost her son; she'll feel like she gained a daughter, as clichéd as that may sound.

7. GIVE IT SOME TIME
You can't expect your mother-in-law to embrace you and form a close bond the minute you come back from the honeymoon. Like any other healthy relationship, it's going to take a little time. But if you work toward it, gradually, you and your mother-in-law will – gasp! – enjoy each other's company in a matter of months.

8.AVOID COMPETITION
If you want to know how to get along with your mother-in-law, avoid competing with her at all costs! If your husband considers her the best cook in the world, let it be and don't try to one-up her by trying to be the new best cook in the family. Remember that there is room for both of you in your man's life so don't feel like you have to outdo her in any way or feel threatened by her. Your husband fell in love with you for a reason, not because you're a carbon copy of his mom!

9.BE CLEAR
One of the most valuable lessons to learn in how to get along with your mother-in-law is to be open and be clear in communicating. You don't have to tolerate anyone criticising you or your family, so don't feel like she can get away with saying whatever she wants. At the same time, be sure the two of you are communicating effectively and that you clarify any misunderstandings that may occur.

Misunderstandings can really ruin relationships so make sure you always clear things up and clear the air!

Becoming part of a new family can be challenging but there are definitely ways to make it work and lots of useful ways to charm your mother-in-law! Remember that she was once in your position too so try to put yourself in her shoes and do your best to get along with your new family! Who knows? If you follow these tips, you might even become your mother-in-law's favourite child.

1. "Good evening woman of God Dr Jennifer Irungu, greetings from Kenya. My name is Christabel. I am privileged to be on the powerful platform of Girls Talk live and I have a testimony to give.

Since I joined Girls Talk late last year nothing about me has remained the same. God has used you mightily to transform my life as a woman and as a wife. When I joined my marriage was young and under attack. My husband and I were not in good terms and he would not want to hear anything about children. When I posted this, I got very good feedback from the precious ladies around the world on GT. You prayed for me and today I am six weeks pregnant, due September. Through your prayers my marriage is awesome and my husband is so excited about the baby. I give God all the Glory. You're indeed powerfully anointed. I bless God for you and I say a big thank you mum. Asante."

2. "Mind blowing awesome experience with GIRLS TALK today in London! As a pastor, it helped me to overcome some hidden issues in my life. I fully recommend other senior pastors' wives to come and partake of this wisdom, so their church members' marriages will be saved. You are such a vital tool for such a time like this in the world. Thank you, Dr. Jennifer and your team. I believe I receive my warfare has ended."

3. "God bless you Dr. Jennifer because of Girls Talk teachings. I was so embarrassed about my problem that I did

not even want to talk to my doctor about it. But it was ruining my life. I was so self-conscious about it, especially around my husband. Every time we were starting to get intimate, I'd always pull away and run to the bathroom. Even though I had just taken a shower hours before, I'd always wash up again with a wet cloth, and checking to make sure he wouldn't notice. Sometimes I'd even spray myself with perfume. But now am free after using the natural yogurt. Love you, love you, so much Woman of God. You mean so much to many tormented women. Continue this good work you are doing."

4. "Morning Mum, thank you so very much for sending a voice mail prayer. I had been sleeping then something told me to check my phone, when I did, I saw the prayer you posted on Girls Talk and I just started praying it until I found myself sleeping. This morning at 6 am I listened to your voice mail prayer I felt this force enter me and I started crying heavily and then fell asleep, now I feel so much peace upon me and feel revived. Thank you for meeting me at my point of need in prayer mum." Love you. D. Hillary

5. "Good day Dr. Jennifer. I have a testimony; do you remember when I had a chart with you about how I was so dry down there, and you advised me that washing myself with yoghurt helps? Dr Jennifer I have washed only twice and for a long time I have been using something else, believe you me this week I have been so wet without using any no medication. My husband has been asking me what I have done. Dr Jennifer God has used you to change lives not only spiritually, but even physically and emotionally. I thank God for your life, you are a chosen woman of God. Be blessed and highly favoured. Thank you so much."

- Clean the Chosen room neatly
- Make sure that there are no photos on the wall
- Sanctify that special place or room
- Place a clean mat, cloth or carpet
- Place a Bible there for reference
- Place a book and a pen
- The Confession book
- Your Prayer points
- Your Prophetic Scriptures
- Write your vision down and place it on your altar.
- You can Pray, kneel, prostrate, lift hands in this special place or room.
- It's your special place to meet God and communicate with God.
- Expect angelic visitations. Mighty Revelation and vision revealed here.
- Whatever may be troubling you, write it down and put it on the altar.

Matthew 14:23

And when he had sent the multitudes away, he went up into a mountain apart to pray: and when the evening was come, he was there alone.

MARRIAGE FIRE PRAYER POINTS

1. Every evil seducer from hell must be exposed and die by fire.

2. Every devil's agent in form of friends, in-laws and outlaws, expected and unexpected visitors, family members, anyone who has taken it upon themselves to break our marriages MUST DIE BY FIRE. The word of God says let no one put asunder what God has joined together. The scriptures cannot be broken. Anyone trying to break our marriages must die by fire.

3. Any woman intending to take my God given husband, any woman having an affair with my husband right now I take authority in Jesus' name I break that fake demonic relationship. I decree it shall not stand. The bible says the power of life and death is in the tongue. Today we speak death to that extra marital relationship we command it to die by fire. We destroy every soul tie between our husbands and those PLAN- B Women.

4. Pray for the fire of God to be ignited afresh in your marriage that there may be more love like never before.

5. Cancel every evil association your husband gets involved in.

6. Bring down every demonic alter raised up against your marriage.

7. Cancel every negative word spoken on your wedding day, over your wedding rings, wedding clothes, wedding food, wedding venue. Cancel it in Jesus' name.

8. We come against every spirit of rejection, divorce, separation die by fire. My husband and I will always work together like Aquila and Priscilla.

9. We come against the spirit of foolish arguments, sulking and fault finding in our marriages. We command it to die by fire.

10. Anything, anyone that my husband gets involved that does not glorify God or is not in my interest and favour die by fire.

11. We cover all areas of our marriages with the blood of Jesus. The Bible says the blood of Jesus speaks better things than the blood of Abel. It will better love intimacy and all that pertains to us.

12. Let us thank God because He has heard our prayer and the victory is ours in Jesus' name Amen.

1. Pray that spirit of singleness be broken in your life.

2. Bind every negative word ever spoken in your life even before you were born.

3. Break every generational curse of singleness from your mother's house and father's house, break its hold over your life. Command it to die by fire.

4. Bring down every demonic alter raised against you. The Bible says we fight not against flesh and blood but against principalities, rulers and evil spirits in high places.

5. Bind every spell cast on you. Break its power. No weapon forged against you shall prosper. Isaiah 54:17

6. Bind every Prince of Persia standing between you and your Boaz.

7. Wherever they took your pictures, personal clothing or belonging; send holy ghost fire to consume them.

8. Confess and ask God for forgiveness. Anything you might have done /said knowing or unknowingly that is hindering you from accessing your future husband.

9. By faith wipe your future husband's face with the blood of Jesus. Remove any demonic veil that is causing him not to see you. Tear it in Jesus' name.

10. Pray that your God given Boaz shall not be found by any other woman.

11. Begin to remove every garment of shame that the enemy has put over your life.

12. Bind every spirit of rejection. Command it to die by fire.

13. Pray that the word of God moulds you to be a proverbs 31 woman.

14. Pray for God to remove anything that is not of Him / unworthy that is blocking you from your future husband.

15. Pray for the spirit of discernment to know your right man.

16. Cover your future husband that he will be invisible to the eyes of the enemy out there.

17. Pray for God to cleanse, sanctify, and bless you so you will be like a sweet-smelling aroma to your future husband.
18. Cancel every spirit of unnecessary delay.

19. Pray against evil desire. That you and your Boaz will abstain from any sexual activity till you are married.

20. By faith pray and sanctify your future marriage bed. That it shall not be defiled. That only you and your hubby will sleep in it.

21. Pray for your future sex life. That both you and your husband will derive pleasure from each other and you will satisfy each other needs.

22. Pray for your husband that he will not lust after any other woman. Only you will quench his sexual thirst.

23. Bind every spirit of good beginning and bad ending

24. Take authority over anyone covered in sheepskin disguising themselves as potential Boaz. Command them to be exposed and die by fire.

25. Every devil agent intending to come and confuse and use you then dump you must be exposed.

26. Begin to pray for your future home, in laws, and all your husband relatives that you will be an epitome of peace. That any devil agent in that home assigned to cause you havoc must die by fire.

27. Begin to pray for your wedding day that no devil agent will make it to the venue. Pray for God's will to prevail.

28. Pray for financial provision for both your wedding and marriage life as a couple. That you will never struggle for anything. You will never lack.

29. Pray against spirit of divorce and separation between you and your future husband. You will live happily and enjoy your marriage.

30. Thank God for victory. Thank Him for answered prayer. Thank Him for that good looking man. Thank Him for that beautiful wedding day. Thank Him for being God in your life.

PRAYER POINTS FOR THOSE BELIEVING GOD FOR THE FRUIT OF THE WOMB

1. Take authority over the spirit of bareness. Bind it command it to die by fire. Exodus 23:26 None will miscarry, none will be barren.

2. Cancel every negative and idle word ever spoken over your life. Render it helpless and powerless over your life. Declare you are fruitful. Psalms 128:3 your wife will be like a fruitful vine within your house, your sons will be like olive shoots around your table.

3. Speak to your reproductive system, speak to your ovaries, speak to those blocked fallopian tubes. Command them to open up in Jesus' name.

4. Speak to that irregular menstrual cycle. The Bible says God is God of order. He did not create that irregular cycle in you. He made everything perfect. Speak to that irregular cycle command it to line up in Jesus' name. Command it to become regularly just like God created it to be.

5. Take authority over lack of ovulation.

Command your reproductive system to begin to ovulate.
6. Take authority over any fibroids, cysts or any growth in your womb that is making it impossible for you to conceive. Plead the blood of Jesus over your womb. Let it wash and destroy anything that is not of God.

7. Take authority right now over any ritual that they may have performed on you, on your body, on your FIRST MENSTRUAL BLOOD. Denounce that ritual in Jesus' name. Detach yourself from it in Jesus' name. Cancel any incantation they said over you. Render it powerless over your life.

8. Send the angel on assignment to wherever they buried your menstrual blood, body parts (hair, nails, skin), inner clothing. Send Holy ghost fire to burn all witchcraft connected to you. Declare I am free from every stronghold of witchcraft in Jesus' name.

9. Repent of any sin you might have engaged in knowingly or unknowingly that activates/activated this spirit of bareness. Ask God to cleanse you and give you a fresh start. The blood of Jesus washes white as snow.

10. Take authority in the name of Jesus and bring down any alter that they have raised up against you. Send Holy ghost fire to consume it.

11. Take authority over every generational curse from your father's house, your mother's house that is following you, command it to die by fire. Render it helpless and powerless over your life.

12. Take authority over any spirit of miscarriages. Bind it in the name of Jesus. Command it to loose its grip over your womb. Command it to die by fire.

13. Take authority over any curse they spoke over you directly or indirectly. Declare it shall not come to pass. Jesus has set you free.

14. Bind every negative YOU ever spoken to YOURSELF. Render it helpless and powerless over your life. Command it to die by fire.

15. Take authority over any blood disease that is activating bareness. Command it to die by fire. Plead the blood of Jesus over your life.

16. Take authority over any diabolical food they fed you in a dream to make you barren. Plead the blood of Jesus to wash it out. Command Holy Ghost fire to burn it all.

17. Take authority over all monitoring spirits assigned to monitor your progress in conception. Ask the Lord to strike them blind in Jesus' name.

18. Take authority over every Peninnah spirit assigned to mock you and cause you to lose hope and focus. Command it to die by fire.

19. Whosoever is behind your shame, ask God to expose them. That they will not rest until they confess to you publicly where they went and what they did to you.

20. By Faith begin to see yourself carrying your baby. BEGIN TO CALL OUT YOUR BABIES BY THEIR NAMES. Command them to come forth to you in Jesus' name.

21. Begin to thank God because your prayers have been heard. You will carry your baby to term. Thank God because

your Samuel is here. Your Isaac is here in Jesus' name. You will hear the cries of your own baby. Thank God because your baby shower is here.

1. Take authority in the name of Jesus right now, cover your children with the blood of Jesus. Plead the blood of Jesus over their mind, will and emotions.

2. Decree and declare that no weapon forged against them shall prosper.

3. Cancel every negative assignment in their life and destiny. Render it helpless and powerless. Return in back to sender.

4. Right now send the angels to remove any traps they may have set up for them both in the spiritual and physical realm.

5. Take authority right now against All/Any devil agents they may come into contact with in play groups, schools, colleges / university, social media, hospital, recreational centres, churches and many more. Ask the Lord to put a hedge of fire around them. Ask the Holy spirit to give them wisdom to know what to say. That they will not fall in the trap of collecting anything from them.

6. In the name of Jesus cancel every mark the enemy might have put on your child to set them aside for initiation into the kingdom of darkness. Plead the blood of Jesus over their life. Wipe off that demonic mark by faith with the blood of Jesus. Declare SEVEN TIMES: EVERY DEMONIC ACCESS TO MY CHILD IS DENIED. MY CHILD IS MARKED FOR

GREATNESS. HE/ SHE WILL SERVE THE LORD JESUS
FOR THE REST OF HIS/ HER LIFE.

7. Take authority against any witchcraft performed on your
child whilst the umbilical cord was being cut. Cancel every
incantation made during birth. Render every negative and
idle word spoken powerless in Jesus' name. Send fire of the
Holy Ghost to wherever they buried the umbilical cord.
Command the fire of God to burn every witchcraft buried
with it.

8. Take authority over every negative and idle word spoken
over your kids even before they were born. Bind those words.
Command them to die by fire.

9. Take authority over every evil eye watching your child's
progress. Command the Lord to strike it blind. Every
monitoring spirit die by fire.

10. Take authority over any evil plans, thoughts or desire to
join gangs, cults, consuming and peddling drugs, joining
terror groups, extremists, watching pornography, radicalism,
anything that is not of God. Bind those plans. Destroy and
smash that desire. Declare my children will not have such
negative thoughts. Cover their minds with the blood of Jesus.

11. Take authority over spirit of fear and depression
depriving your child the chance to be happy. Bind that spirit.

12. Take authority over the spirit of mental decapitation.
Declare my child has the mind of Christ and just like Daniel
he/she will excel far above his/her peers.

13. Take authority over every sickness and disease that is causing your child prolonged periods of absence from school. Bind that sickness. Declare by the stripes of Jesus my child was healed.

14. Take authority over stubborn spirit, unruly spirit, defiant attitude, controlling spirit, anger, spirit of heaviness, bind these spirits. Command them to leave your child.

15. Bind every spirit of confusion assigned to your kids. Send it back to sender.

16. Bind every spirit of death attached and assigned to your child. Command it to die by fire. Your children will not die young. They will live to a ripe age.

17. Pray for the people your kids get into contact with i.e., teachers, classmates, playmates, bus drivers, passengers, shopkeepers, doctors etc. Pray that no familiar spirit in the form of any one of these people will come into contact with your kids.

18. Take authority over any diabolical food they might have fed them in your absence, in the dream or even in the physical. Cancel its hold over your child.
Take authority over any alter they may have raised against your child. Bring it down.

19. Declare right now wherever they took your child's pictures, hair, name, nails, skin, clothes to rob them of their God given destiny, May the fire of God burn all that witchcraft now in Jesus' name. Ask the Holy Ghost to revel where they buried it and who did this to you. Declare that witchcraft null and void over your child.

20. Come against any disagreement you may be having with your children which is causing division. Denounce that lie of the devil to separate you and your children. Bind every scattering spirit.

21. Come against every spirit of hatred that makes you hate your own children and vice versa. Render it powerless over your family. Declare you and your children will be bound with cords of love that can never be broken.

22. Come against every spirit of disagreement between you and your children.

23. Come against every spirit of madness assigned to your kids. Declare my child has the mind of Christ.

24. Pray against vagabond spirit that causes your child to wander aimlessly

25. Pray against that demon that causes your child/ children to run away from home. Bind it in Jesus' name. BEGIN TO CALL BACK YOUR CHILD/CHILDREN BY THEIR NAMES. SEND ANGELS ON ASSIGNMENT TO LOCATE AND BRING THEM HOME.

26. Take authority against evil family members who misguide our children or turn them against us. Ask God to expose them. Declare they shall not have peace till they confess.

27. Plead the blood of Jesus over your kids as they leave for school, abroad, play group, etc that they shall leave and come back safe.

28. Begin to thank God because He has heard your prayers concerning your kids. They will be excellent. They will do you proud. Isaiah 8:18 Here am I and the children the Lord has given me; we are signs and symbols in Israel from the Lord Almighty who dwells in in mount Zion.

Finally declare over your kids 11 B's that they are BLESSED. BRIGHT. BRILLIANT. BOLD. BEAUTIFUL. BRAVE. BEST. BUSINESS MINDED. BILLIONAIRE. BOSS & BARRIER BREAKERS.

.

HOW TO INSPIRE GREAT MANNERS IN YOUR CHILDREN

1. When entering the house greet your children or even hug them. This should help develop their sense of love and self-worth. (2 Samuel 6:20)

2. Be good to your neighbours and never backbite. Never speak ill of other drivers when on the road. Your children would listen, absorb and emulate. (Luke 6:46)

3. When calling your parents, encourage your children to speak to them. When visiting your parents take your children with you. The more they see you take care of your parents the more they will learn to take care of you. (Ephesians 6:2)

4. When driving them to school, don't always play albums or CDs in the car. Rather, tell them some motivational stories yourself. This will have a greater impact - trust me! (Deuteronomy 6: 7, 11:19)

5. Read to them a short story and even a scripture a day – it doesn't take much time, but very impactful in creating strong bonds and wonderful memories. (Genesis 18:19)

6. Comb your hair, clean your teeth and wear presentable cloths even if sitting at home and not going out for the day. They need to learn that being clean and tidy has nothing to do with going out!

7. Try not to blame or comment on every word or action they say or do. Learn to overlook and let go sometimes. This certainly builds their self-confidence.

8. Ask your children's permission before entering their rooms. Don't just knock and enter, but then wait for a verbal permission. They will learn to do the same when wanting to enter your room.

9. Apologise to your children if you made a mistake. Apologising teaches them to be humble and polite. (Proverbs 22:4)

10. Don't be sarcastic or make fun of their views or feelings, even if you "didn't mean it" and was "only joking". It really hurts.

11. Show respect to your children's privacy. It's important for their sense of value and self-esteem.

12. Don't expect that they will listen or understand the first time. Don't take it personal. But be patient and consistent. (Acts 26:3)

13. Pray with them. Show them how to pray. Lead by example. Then ask them to lead too on their turn. (Luke 11:2)

14. In addition, ask them to discuss their daily plans after the morning prayers. Children without concrete daily plans usually join others in executing theirs. They fall easy to peer pressure.

15. Hold them and bless them specially every morning. Don't let them leave your house without your blessings. Anoint

their heads and prophesy. Command their star to shine that
day.

IMPORTANT POINTS TO CELEBRATE YOUR CHILD'S BIRTHDAY

BREAKFAST IN BED: Make a special surprise for your child "breakfast in bed". Serve him/her by singing their favourite song; you could sing it or play it on your phone, iPad or computer. Great songs on YouTube.

WISH YOUR CHILD A VERY BIG HAPPY BIRTHDAY: Bless him or her and tell her or him that this is your special day made just for you by God to REJOICE! Encourage your child to enjoy himself or herself in the lord.

PROPHESY & DECLARE:
Prophesy to him or her, "My child I prophesy to you;
You are Blessed, Bright, Brilliant, Bold,
Beautiful, Brave, Best, Business minded, Billionaire, Boss,
& Barrier Breaker forever in Jesus' name."

READ BIBLE TOGETHER: Read the Bible Scriptures for Birthday together: Isaiah 54:13. Isaiah 8:18, Psalms 127:3-5, 1 Sam 2:26. Etc.

SOW A SEED ACCORDING TO HIS/ HER AGE:
According to your country's currency where you are. Thank God for all those years. Amen.

GO OUT OR PREPARE A GREAT SPECIAL MEAL:
Celebrate with family together. Amen.

Ladies on Fire
93 Camberwell Station Road, London, SE5 9JJ
England, United Kingdom
Tel: +44 207 738 3668 (UK)
Tel: 1 347 708 1449 (USA)
Email: drjennifer@ladiesonfire.org

Yes Dr Jennifer! I want to come into agreement with you that as I sow this seed according to the number of my age, I will receive a physical manifestation of powerful miracles in every area of my life.

I have enclosed my best gift of £_____

Here is my Prayer Request covering the 7 areas I would like the Lord to manifest His miracles in my life:

_____

_____

_____

_____

_____

_____

_____

_____

_____

_____

(Continued on Back)

141

Name:

_____

Address:

_____
_____
_____
_____
_____
_____
_____

Telephone:

_____

Email:

_____

ABOUT DR JENNIFER

First Lady of the Kingdom Church and President of Ladies on Fire, this is the woman of God behind the powerful, lifechanging ministry of The Kingdom Church and Bishop Climate Ministries. A powerful woman of God, anointed with extra-ordinary wisdom for women. Dr. Jennifer is a devoted wife to Bishop Climate and a loving mother of four children. She epitomizes the virtuous woman mentioned in Proverbs 31. She is a constant source of love and support to Bishop, The Kingdom Church members and partners. She has committed herself to birth strength to all church members. Her humility, warmth and genuine love for God and people have led to her counselling and touching many lives. Her anointing towards women is incredible and continue bringing great healing and restoration to many through her ministry LADIES ON FIRE MINISTRY. She travels the world to speak to and empower women of all ages hosting a number of conventions each year in cities across the World. Many families, businesses and individuals around the world have been impacted by ladies on fire international conferences.

Dr. Jennifer's dynamic teaching style and practical approach to ministry have ministered to millions over the years on topics that range from Christian family and biblical prosperity to character development.

She has written 7 powerful best-selling books and is well known by her TV programs on Sky digital TV, Ladies on Fire 24 Internet TV, DVDs and audio CDs. Also known by her 3 phenomenal Ladies on Fire International Conferences in UK and Africa (Catch the Fire Conference, Unforgettable Woman Conference and Esther Banquet conference).

Why not join us at an upcoming conference in your area?
Follow her on Facebook, Twitter and YouTube
drjennifer@bishopclimate.org
drjennifer@ladiesonfire.org
firstladytkc@yahoo.co.uk
www.bishopclimate.org
www.ladiesonfire.org
Tel: +44 01315552290
Tel: +44 02077383668

OTHER BOOKS BY THE AUTHOR

Power of Confession
How To Sanctify Your Home
21 Days Daniel Fasting
A-Z Women in the Bible
The Proverbs 31 Woman
Queens & Queen Mothers In The Bible
How To Take Communion At Home

To order more books or for more resources on Communion and taking it at home, please call our prayer line today.

Tel: +44 207 738 3668 (UK)
Tel: 1 347 708 1449 (USA)

Printed in Great Britain
by Amazon